Reflections of Body Image in Art Therapy

Reflections of Body Image in Art Therapy

Exploring Self through Metaphor and Multi-Media

Margaret R. Hunter

Foreword by Dr. Richard Carolan

Jessica Kingsley *Publishers*
London and Philadelphia

All artwork featured is printed with kind permission from the artists.
Photographs of artwork are printed with kind permission from Gary Powell.

First published in 2012
by Jessica Kingsley Publishers
116 Pentonville Road
London N1 9JB, UK
and
400 Market Street, Suite 400
Philadelphia, PA 19106, USA

www.jkp.com

Library of Congress Cataloging in Publication Data
A CIP catalog record for this book is available from the Library of Congress

British Library Cataloguing in Publication Data
A CIP catalogue record for this book is available from the British Library

ISBN 978 1 84905 892 6
eISBN 978 0 85700 610 3

Printed and bound in the United States

To my mother, Marjorie, and my granddaughter, Adelina Rose.
You are the bookends of my life story.

Contents

Foreword

The human experience is often characterized as a journey, with the body understood as the vehicle allowing passage. Less clear is who it is that we identify as the passenger, and the boundary that distinguishes the passenger from the vehicle.

When I walk to the mirror, I intend to see myself. When I cross paths with acquaintances, they are certain that it is me that they see. Yet when I walk in unknown neighborhoods, or scan the world of television or digital reality, I see vehicles, bodies, and imagine passengers.

It is said that our concept of self is based to a very considerable degree upon our assumptions about how others perceive us, and that we very seldom, almost never, verify these assumptions.

When I walk to the mirror, I intend to see myself, but I assess my vehicle. I am trying to see myself, but alas, the vehicle is the lens that I am looking through.

Who crafted this lens? The eyes of this vehicle, what assumptions formed their focus? What serves as the set of instructions for perception and judgement as I approach the mirror?

Ellen Dissanayake, in her remarkable text *Homo Aestheticus*, states that "the natural body serves as the canvas for the imposition of cultural designs" (1992, p.109).

These are the waters that Margaret Hunter has set her course through in this beautiful text. She navigates through mirror and lens and culture. The journey of the human experience throughout history is most accurately portrayed through metaphor. This is the language that Margaret uses as a set of instructions for developing navigation skills and lens cleaning. She moves through the theoretical to the practical.

In this text, Margaret combines the empathetic understanding of a practitioner who has metaphorically held the hand of many women with faulty lenses impoverished through the imposition of cultural designs, and guided them with the clinician's understanding of the complexity of navigation. There is no directive, no recommendation, no navigational strategy in this book that Margaret has not developed through the experience of many workshops, with many women travelers as expert witnesses.

This book is designed for all women on the journey; it is also designed for their guides. Art is a very powerful navigational instrument. It is also a toy with which we should all play. Margaret writes in a manner that invites play, yet also honors the possibilities of these toys as primary navigational instruments in the journey of the human experience. We should all play; guides should be very well versed in the richness and complexities of art as a navigational instrument.

Margaret, in this book, invites women to open their purses, consider their mirrors and try on new shoes. She supports them in noticing the blades of grass in concrete walkways, and approaching the tree of life. She facilitates a dialogue with "Barbie" and invites all women to become the captain of their ship. More than that, she offers navigational plans for the journey. All of this inspired by a walk on the beach, and a look in the mirror. Enjoy your journey.

Dr. Richard Carolan
Graduate Art Therapy Psychology Department
Notre Dame de Namur University, Belmont, CA

Acknowledgments

This book represents my ten-year journey as an art therapist working in the field of body image and eating disorder treatment. Many people have traveled this journey with me. Some walked with me for a while; others were constant companions. These people have my deepest gratitude for helping to make this book possible.

I would first like to acknowledge all the women who participated in the art therapy processes described in this book. The images of your artwork, and the personal statements featured throughout the book, enhance the descriptions of the art processes. You showed me what courage really looks like, as you accepted the call to adventure. Like all journeys, this one was not always easy. You faced obstacles on the waters and roadways of life, and you supported each other with validation, compassion and honesty. Your tears and laughter echo off each and every page of this book. You have my deepest gratitude.

I will always remember Bertha. Her donated purses, shoes, gloves and miscellaneous "cool" objects helped so many women in their process of healing. The memory of your life and spirit lives on in the art.

There were several women who stood with me as I launched out on my maiden voyage. Cindy Duenas would not take "I don't think so" for an answer when she approached me to facilitate a body image support group. I think Cindy saw my path before I did. Corrina Lindblom stepped forward to walk with me as we co-facilitated our first adolescent body image support group. Corrina brought creative energy and ideas that significantly impacted my own development.

I met Signe Darpinian along the road of life. Signe carried a light of hope for people affected by eating disorders. She opened the doors to Meghan's Place Eating Disorder Center in Central Valley, CA, so that weary travelers could find a place to rest. Many of the art processes in this book were developed in my work at Meghan's Place.

Every traveler on the road of life needs a guide. Dr. Richard Carolan walked with me as I began to conceptualize this book. I looked to him for direction when I felt lost on the road; he always carried a compass and a map. His calm, reassuring voice during our weekly telephone consultations helped me to remain steadily on course.

My colleagues at California State University, Stanislaus, provided support and encouragement along the way. Dr. Daniel Berkow, Sharon Powell, Renae Floyd, Jodie Nullmeyer and Ona Baker read material and responded with valuable critiques. I am grateful for their patience and generous feedback.

My early mentors, Dr. Leslie Ross, Dr. Sharon Gocke and Dr. Arnell Etherington, taught me the value of exploring images, symbols and stories; using reason, emotion and imagination. You have my respect and gratitude.

My family expressed love and support beyond the spoken word during this book development and writing process. They helped in every way possible. I am grateful for the amazing women in my family who refuse to be defined by cultural stereotypes. You inspire me each and every day. I am grateful to my sister, Eileen, for sacrificing many lunch hours to review material and "get back to me ASAP." Thank you.

Terri Lawson met up with me towards the end of this journey. She helped me carry my written account of this adventure to its final destination. Terri's ability to visualize and organize the many aspects of this project helped to bring it to fruition. Her calm, caring and direct communication gave me hope that this project would be completed. Don Lawson provided creative and practical input that made a difference. I thank you both.

Gary Powell documented the artwork created on this journey. His wonderful images are contained in this book.

Finally, I would like to thank my husband, Mark. We have walked the road of life together for over three decades and I have felt his support every step of the way. Thank you for always encouraging me to look within myself to find my beauty and definition in the world. Take my hand, and let's continue our journey.

Introduction

Every woman has authorship of her own epic story. From the moment she begins her journey, she stands at the helm of her vessel. The waters of life that she sails upon offer life-giving nourishment for her mind, body and spirit. She may have to batten down the hatches of her ship in preparation for restless seas, and extend her sails to greet the sky during stormy times. While sailing upon the waters she will encounter new lands, with foreign people and novel customs.

Women travelers, throughout their lives, have many opportunities for adventures. This is a time in history when women are able to pull up their anchors, and set out to see what life has to offer. When a captain recognizes the abilities and potential of her own ship, she is able to sail upon the seas with direction and purpose. The beacon of light that helps women navigate their ships through darkness and fog is found within. This book takes women on an incredible journey into the light of the imagination, within the realm of metaphors, to explore new definitions of self and the vessel that they travel within. Cultural standards and expectations, particularly related to body image, are rigorously challenged with positive, self-affirming images and statements. Women learn that perception of body is significantly affected by integration of interpersonal and cultural projections. Relaxation and guided imagery, combined with diverse, multi-media art processes, help women deflect these projections, strengthening the connection to the core self that lives beneath the skin.

My own reflective journey began nearly a decade ago as I found myself standing in front of the ocean on the Californian coast, wondering what the beautiful body of water could teach me about life. I recalled the many times that I humbly stood before the power of the great sea, waiting for an epiphany or some type of sign that would direct me on a path towards awakening and transformation. On this day, I performed my usual routine: took off my shoes; felt my toes sink into the sand; looked out to the water, as far as I could see; and waited for something to happen. I think everything began to change when I *accidentally* became aware of my breathing. I suddenly noticed that the air moving in and out of my body was shifting in sync with the rhythm of the ocean waves. My awareness traveled down my body to my toes. I felt the cool, rough texture of the sand and the sudden chill of the water gliding over my feet. My multi-sensory experience on that day culminated in my full presence with the world around me. I wasn't sure how I would use, or develop, this new experience; however, I knew that in some small (or profound) way I had changed. That moment in time marked the beginning of a transformation in my life and would provide a foundation for the body image work I would do for years to come. Women have many qualities in common with the ocean, and have an innate ability to form an imagined, multi-sensory experience of *being like* the ocean. Just as we begin our life in the water of our mother's womb, we begin the journey of reclaiming our lives in the waters of the archetypal womb.

The presentation of ideas in chapter introductions is in line with the overall message of the book: celebration of diversity; joy in connection; and strength to stand alone if needed. Consistent themes and messages connect each chapter to the book as a whole; however, the chapters are not dependent on each other for meaning or value.

Chapter 1 marks the beginning of the voyage of self-discovery. The course is charted as travelers and their guides prepare to set out upon the waters of life. They explore maps in the form of theoretical models so they have direction along the way. A story is introduced in the language of metaphors as preparation for passage into the world of the imagination, where self will be explored in new and creative ways. This chapter briefly explores familial and cultural influences that may affect a woman's perception of her body-vessel. She may doubt the worthiness or reliability of the ship she travels within. Her resistance to the call to adventure is acknowledged as a part of the process, and the benefits of such a journey are introduced. The roles and responsibilities of the guide are clarified.

In Chapter 2, "Lessons from the Ocean," the participants are introduced to a *journey* theme. Anticipation of traveling from one place to another for a vacation or reprieve from the stress of day-to-day living has universal appeal. Actual trips are not always practical or possible. In Chapter 2, the relaxation and guided imagery process helps participants calm their bodies, before tapping creative resources to take a journey within the mind. As soft, instrumental music (with ocean waves) plays in the background, participants focus on breath awareness. With gentle encouragement, they begin to experience their own systems in sync with the rhythm of ocean waves. The guided imagery process takes women to the shores of the ocean, where they experience a multi-sensory connection to the water and immediate surroundings. Women are encouraged to stay present in the moment, fully alive with all their senses. Thoughts and feelings enter the mind, and drift away, like the fluid motion of the ocean waves. The individual takes an imaginary journey by sea into the world of their imagination; a land where thoughts and ideas are expressed through metaphors. This experiential introduces various practices and concepts that flow throughout the book. A brief drawing experiential follows the guided imagery process. Women draw their experience of standing in front of the ocean, allowing thoughts and feelings to move through mind and body.

Once women have been introduced to the ocean as an important and relatable symbol, they continue their life journeys by sailing upon the "Waters of Life." The guided imagery process in Chapter 2 leads into the Chapter 3 art process where travelers move from the ocean shores, into the waters of life. When I was a child I accompanied my mother on trips to Monterey and Bodega Bay. Often, we stopped to look at the ships in the docks and on the water. I was always amazed at how similar the boats appeared to be in basic structure and color; yet they also seemed so diverse because of the personal details added by the owners. During this experiential, participants are introduced to a variety of art materials used to create boats for the journey. Each member folds a basic, white, origami boat and then embellishes it to reflect unique physical, emotional and spiritual qualities of self. An anchor is created to establish a sense of stability should the boat encounter turbulent waters, or begin to drift without direction on the sea. The relaxation and guided imagery process invites participants to reflect upon qualities of their boat; and therefore, qualities of the self. Participants work together in small groups to imagine and create the "Waters of Life." Each woman places her boat in the water to begin her *maiden voyage*. A safe and validating space is established and maintained for the dialogue and reflection process that follows. Women are given the opportunity to express any thoughts, ideas or feelings they experience in this process.

The first experiential chapters prepare women for their journeys by guiding them into a relaxed state with a non-judgemental awareness of being present in the moment. The stress that women carry with them as they travel along the road of life is lifted for a while, and they are able to explore their internal worlds with confidence that they can manage thoughts and emotions that are experienced. The Chapter 4 experiential is like a resting stop along the road, a type of aid station. During this brief resting period, women are asked to consider potential risks and benefits of continuing along the road of self-discovery. They are reminded of the skills that they have learned along the way; and are reassured that they will continue to draw from internal resources and support from the group environment. Participants discuss heroes from history and contemporary culture, with particular focus on female heroes. We consider the broad definition of the concept of hero: mythological creatures who are capable of extraordinary feats; modern, supernatural figures who dominate video and computer games; and mere mortals who act bravely in the face of danger and significant risk.

The journey of the hero truly came alive for me when my eighth grade class read a simplified version of the epic poem, *The Odyssey*. I was fascinated by the adventures of Odysseus; amazed, really, at his ability to face and overcome obstacles that were unimaginable. I found the story extremely intriguing; however, I could not apply the deeper meaning to my own life at the time. During high school, I became interested in Joseph Campbell's monomyth, "the hero's journey" (Campbell, 2008). At this age I could (and did) imagine myself as a heroine, traveling bravely through a world that I often feared. Like most of my peers, I stopped to consider risks to some degree; however, I often moved forward with a kind of blind faith that somehow I would live on, no matter what. Adolescence may be a difficult and painful time in our lives; however, we go through it, and survive, for a reason. Those critical years help to prepare us for the challenges we face ahead. We are oblivious to our own hero development during this important developmental stage.

Women may show healthy resistance to returning to a time in life that was driven by impulsivity and a disregard for mortality; however, if a woman does allow herself to return to the memories of her youth, she finds the remains of those days in the courage that she felt, and the faith she relied upon as she moved forward. In Chapter 5, the woman traveling the road of self-discovery mapped out in this book will pause for a rest. She will search for, and find, that brave young woman inside of herself; that part that is always there, waiting to be called upon. She hears the call to adventure, and she must decide if she will go on. If she chooses to go forward, she will create a heroine's wand to carry with her. The wand gives her strength, and serves as a reminder that she is never alone.

Once participants choose to move ahead on the road to self-discovery, they prepare for the journey by packing the skills they have learned and practiced. The backpack for the trip should not be so full and heavy that it becomes cumbersome to carry; however, essential items make the trip more enjoyable and help to manage and overcome problems encountered along the way. The skills introduced in Chapter 5 fortify the traveler and give her confidence that she can face whatever lies ahead. When I was 16 years old, and learning to drive a car, I realized that I was unable to follow directions when they were spoken in the language of cardinal points. I found myself pausing with hesitation and fear that I would move in the wrong direction. I lacked a strong internal compass and was relieved and re-energized when I saw the external compass that my dad placed on the dashboard of the car. Women may find themselves stuck in the middle of an emotional state, particularly if the feelings are fueled by negative thoughts. In Chapter 5, travelers develop an internal compass in the form of a "Visual Rating Scale." As women increase their ability to identify primary and secondary emotions, rate the intensity of the emotions in their current experience and identify environmental factors that influence the emotions, they are able to establish a direction of movement. A woman practices the skills that she carries in her backpack; she allows the thoughts and feelings to move through her mind and body, like *waves of the ocean*. As the intensity of the emotion diminishes, she returns to a calmer state, and is able to act with greater clarity and confidence.

As a woman navigates her ship upon the waters of life, she may decide to pull her ship into port and walk along the *roads of life* for a while. Women carry their purses as functional accessories to hold personal belongings. A woman's purse tells the world something about who she is, a story within a story. Several years ago my colleague Signe Darpinian donated several boxes of vintage purses for an art workshop. Her grandmother, Bertha, had acquired the purses during her amazing life journey. As I held each purse, I gathered a sense of who she was, and how she walked through the world. I felt sadness that I would never know this graceful, dignified and stylish woman who had carried these purses through life. The few items remaining inside of the purses also helped to tell her story. During the experiential in Chapter 6, each woman explores a variety of purses and chooses one that she feels a connection to. She carries the purse with her through the workshop, and develops it as a representation of self. The process begins with relaxation and guided imagery to reinforce the experience of acknowledging thoughts and feelings, and allowing them to move through mind and body. This practice builds confidence that even difficult emotions accompanying memories from childhood can be managed. Women from the past are remembered; purses that they carried are brought to life in a multi-sensory experience. Participants then develop their chosen purses, inside and out, to reflect internal and external qualities of self. They are supported in speaking the language of positive self-evaluation; a language they will speak with increasing confidence as they travel on their journey.

In Chapter 7, the relationship between *shoes and self* is explored as an enigmatic association that becomes fully revealed in the creative process, rather than in the explanation of the process. Women require shoes to cover their feet as they move along the roadways of life. Shoes provide balance, stability, protection and warmth. They help *ground* a traveler to the earth, and connect her to the world that she walks through. Shoes, like purses, tell a story about the woman who wears them. They are also the *holders* of the experiences that she has lived through; they see the woman living through these experiences from a unique perspective. Creative development of shoes as a means to explore body image evolved naturally, without planning. It began at a gathering of women who had recently attended the purse workshop and were discussing the possibility of an exhibition. They sat in the art studio, waiting for the meeting to begin. Attention shifted to the several boxes of shoes that had been donated for art processes. The women began to sort through the containers, holding up shoes for others to see while wondering out loud about the people who had worn them. The atmosphere in the room was alive with expressions of curiosity, creativity, laughter and a wide range of other emotions. The women were in accessory mode, having recently developed purses as representations of self. In a unanimous and enthusiastic consensus, they declared their intent to develop shoes to wear through their journey of self-discovery. In what seemed like an afterthought, the women extended an invitation for me to facilitate the process and I gladly accepted. The relationship between *shoes and self* is an enigmatic association that becomes fully revealed in the creative process, rather than in the explanation of the process. Development of shoes in the creative process initiates recall of ages and stages in life; promotes associations with relationships and roles on the life journey; and provides a new perspective of self, specifically related to body image. Travelers are reminded that they carry skills with them to help manage emotions associated with exploration of self, particularly the physical self.

Women meet other people and objects as they sail over the oceans, and walk along the roads of life. Some objects are representations of people—particularly the dolls introduced to girls at an early age. Women of all ages and backgrounds relate to the iconic Barbie doll; she traveled part of the journey of life with our mothers and grandmothers. As a child growing up in the 60s, I was oblivious to developing feminist concerns relating to the objectification of Barbie. I spent hours on the floor of my room, locked in the world of imagination with Barbie and her accessories. I placed her in different situations, surrounded by new environments and interesting people. I became her fashion designer, her hairdresser, her secretary and her *voice*. I spoke for her as she talked with friends, boyfriends, family members, co-workers, bosses and teachers. In my world, Barbie experienced a full range of emotions. She laughed and cried; worried about day-to-day problems; and looked to the future with hopes and fears. As an adult woman, I too developed concerns regarding the stereotypical and unrealistic body size that Barbie has always maintained. In an era marked by body dissatisfaction and body harm, it would be careless to ignore the cultural influence of the plastic doll. During the Chapter 8 "Barbie Speaks" workshop, women bring Barbie to life in the art process, giving her a symbolic voice to speak to critical issues that impact our world. She reflects on her 50 years of life and addresses the pressures she has faced to remain young, thin and stylish. She talks about her relationships; hopes and dreams; her likes and dislikes. Barbie is able to mirror back projections of the woman who is engaging in creative, imaginary play with her.

By the time women reach Chapter 9, they have journeyed a long way on the waters of life and the road to self-discovery. They have developed and practiced skills related to emotion regulation, self-evaluation, and reaching out for support. These travelers carry techniques that help them feel grounded in the moment they are in, incorporating their surroundings into a multi-sensory experience. They know that emotional and/or physical discomfort can be managed with relaxation and guided imagery; they are able to soothe and calm the system while standing at the helm of their ship, or walking along the road. These women travelers have journeyed into the world of the imagination where thoughts and ideas are perceived and expressed in metaphors. The imagination is also a woman's safe place where she can go to find rest. Travelers have been encouraged to express thoughts, feelings and ideas to other women encountered along the way. The wands that a woman creates and carries with her are a reminder of the heroine that lies within, the brave young woman who is waiting to be called upon in times of need. She walks with a heightened awareness that the culture will try to determine her worth. She holds her head high, and looks to her purse as a reminder that she has many qualities of self that help to define who she is in the world. Her shoes carry her along the journey, and help her to look at her body from a new and interesting perspective. She is able to say positive things about herself; and she can do so in the presence of other women. She walks the road, for a short time, with a Barbie doll. The doll reminds the traveler to use her voice, and practice her assertiveness. The traveler is aware that she is part of a greater world community filled with new and interesting cultures that she has yet to discover.

The waters and roads of life pass through familiar territories that women may call home, and foreign lands that are yet to be explored. Women travelers often seek out new experiences in lands with unfamiliar traditions, languages and roles for women. As an undergraduate student I was not able to travel far beyond the immediate horizons outside of my front door. Financial limitations and time restrictions held me to the world I knew; yet my desire to explore culture and history increased rather than diminished. I discovered that I could explore the very diverse lives of people around the world, throughout time, in the colorful pages of art history books. I became particularly interested in the way that artists depict women in their environments, in their roles, and in their bodies. Artists are able to counter pervasive cultural stereotypes by celebrating diversity of personality, spirit and physical form. In the Chapter 9 "Reframe Your Frame" workshop, women enter into a culture of validation and self-appreciation to view themselves with the eyes of an artist. Women use art materials to depict parts of the body that join together to form the whole body. They speak the language of the land, positive descriptive terms about all aspects of self. This chapter contains more information relating to the process than the other chapters. I included this additional information because I found that working directly with the body can evoke a variety of emotional and behavioral responses from participants. Because of this, there are some extra considerations that facilitators should explore ahead of time.

Women are born with an innate connection to the culture of the natural world that surrounds them. As a woman travels along her life journey, she is surrounded by nature, and she is a part of nature. Mother Earth provides inspiration for women as they move along the waters and roads of life: fish and butterflies, birds and animals. She cradles travelers in arms made of grassy valleys, caves and rocky ocean inlets. She provides rest for the weary when the light of the sun moves into the shadows, and sleep comes beneath dark skies painted with stars. Women are introduced to the natural world at an early age. Fairytales, cartoons and nursery rhymes are filled with magical images in nature that bring the stories to life: Cinderella's pumpkin stagecoach, Ariel's underwater world and old Mother Goose herself. My earliest memories from childhood are related to the natural environment of the Pacific Northwest where I grew up. My friends and I spent afternoons lying on the grass, finding shapes in the clouds and human figures amongst the trees. We found pregnant trees, witch trees (with witch hair hanging down) and magical trees that seemed to be waiting for the right moment to come to life. My friend's artist mother came to our class several times a year to facilitate an art project based on the projective nature of trees. We used tissue paper to depict how we saw ourselves as trees during each season of the year; the memory of this art process inspired the "Tree of Life" experiential. During the Chapter 10 workshop, each woman explores her natural identification with a chosen tree. Creative development of a tree as a representation of self is experienced as a non-threatening exploration of body, mind and spirit. This process prepares women for the more direct approach of exploring the body in Chapter 11.

A woman pauses on her journey to explore the unrealistic and potentially unhealthy cultural stereotypes that influence how she perceives herself and, more specifically, how she evaluates her body. Her backpack contains the skills she has learned so far. These techniques help her manage strong emotions associated with self-evaluation. At this stage of her journey she is confident in her ability to reach out to others for support. She is ready to explore how she sees herself when she looks in the mirror. I co-founded Meghan's Place Eating Disorder Center in Central Valley, CA, with my colleague Signe Darpinian in 2004. The image we selected to symbolize the philosophy of our program contains a woman and a mirror. The mirror reflects back two images: one presents the woman in an unhealthy physical state, with dark clouds and rain around her; the other depicts the same woman looking healthy, fully alive and joyful. I encourage women to try to imagine their own appearance in the mirror if they lived a life focused on *health and wholeness*. A woman travels through life in her body-vehicle; and she gets one to last a lifetime. The "Mirror, Mirror" art processes in Chapter 11 promote a new appreciation for the inner workings of the system, with a focus on the communication between mind and body. This process counters self-evaluation based on cultural stereotypes. Women develop a new frame of reference when looking at their image in the mirror. This reference stems from an awakening of a desire to live a healthy, joyful and meaningful life.

Women return to home base to settle in for a while and reflect upon their trip so far. The journey of self-discovery lasts for a lifetime; but the opportunities for adventure offered in this book will soon come to an end. This is an ideal time for a woman to kick off her shoes, set her purse and heroine's wand aside, and get comfortable in her favorite chair. As she lowers the lights, and plays music she loves, she finds herself moving with ease into a state of breath awareness and muscle relaxation. With renewed confidence in her own ability to handle difficult or painful emotions, she thinks about the amazing women she has walked with on this part of her journey, and she imagines herself saying goodbye to each one of them. She reflects upon the validation and support they offered her along the way. She feels ready to begin to assimilate positive qualities of self that she discovered in the creative processes and dialogue and reflection with others. She practices her multi-sensory awareness of being fully present in the moment, in the room, sitting comfortably in her chair. She notices the vase of flowers sitting on her dining room table. She travels easily into the world of the imagination and visualizes different arrangements she could create. How would the bouquet appear if each flower took on a symbolic representation of a quality of self found beneath the skin? What if the vase became the physical body; the holder of all the qualities of self? In Chapter 12, "A Vase of Flowers," the experiential allows women to portray themselves as flowers, with incredible variations of color, form, shape and texture. During this process, women celebrate diversity of the vase/body that is the holder of the flowers. The beauty found in individuality is recognized and reinforced. Women enjoy their vases of flowers as they sit and rest before moving on to the last process on this journey of self-discovery.

As the journey comes to a close in this book, each woman's travels will continue on. Women who have sailed the waters and walked the road of life have developed a deeper appreciation for the body-vehicle that moves them through the storylines of their lives. Each woman knows that her epic life story is made up of short stories. Some of these stories have been lived out and the endings are known; others are just starting to take form in her imagination. During this final experiential in Chapter 13, each participant conceptualizes an *imagined life experience* that she would like to have. She begins her story with a picture, an illustration of the imagined life experience. Women place a photograph of their face or head on paper, and then develop the body that would be needed to fulfill the experience. Women weave together the strengths and limitations of the physical, emotional and spiritual qualities of self that they have explored on this journey. They carry accessories in their backpacks to help manage anxiety associated with actual photographs of self. They see themselves as heroines who answer the call to adventure; they are able to access internal strengths and external support to see them through. I developed this art process years ago when I began working with women who suffered from eating disorders. Often the women felt fearful and stuck, unable to move forward in their life adventure. I found that this experiential awakens hope that all kinds of imagined life experiences are possible. Women appreciate the physical, emotional and spiritual parts of self that work together to create movement on the life journey. As a final reflection and dialogue process, participants share the stories and illustrations of their imagined life experience with fellow travelers. They fully experience the journey in this book coming to an end, while looking forward with hope and confidence to the many stories yet to be lived in *this ongoing journey*.

Some of the artists who participated in the art processes in this book wrote brief summaries of their experiences. Artist statements are found within the chapters. It is our hope that these messages will inspire women to take to the waters and roadways of life, to begin the journey of self-discovery. To preserve anonymity, the names of participants referenced throughout the book have been changed.

TIME
The amount of time allowed for each process in this book varies, depending on the size of the group and the pace of the facilitator. I suggest that facilitators practice reading the relaxation and guided imagery exercises out loud in order to time the reading. Usually 15 minutes is plenty of time; however, the boat process is likely to take longer. I usually plan on 45 minutes for discussion or processing exercises. However, the timing may vary, depending on the size of the group. I allow as much time as possible for the art processes—at least 60–90 minutes.

SECTIONS TO BE READ OUT LOUD
The sections to be read out loud by the facilitator are indicated in bold font with a vertical rule to the left-hand side. I encourage facilitators to read the sections out loud ahead of time in order to develop a pace that suits the process.

ART MATERIALS

During the first art process, I review the art materials on the tables and provide some basic information regarding the materials. Cathy Malchiodi (2007) provides descriptions of materials in *The Art Therapy Sourcebook*. In her book, *Materials and Media in Art Therapy: Critical Understanding of Diverse Artistic Vocabularies*, Catherine Hyland Moon presents helpful descriptions of use of materials in art therapy.

1

Hoisting the Sails

The Journey of Self-Discovery Begins

LIFTING THE WEIGHT OF SADNESS

My journey into the world of body image and art therapy began in response to the growing need for eating disorder prevention and early intervention. A walk in the sand on the ocean shore allowed me to imagine how I might be able to combine my work in the field of body image support and eating disorder treatment, with my passion for art therapy. During my initial travels on the waters and roadways of life, I felt somewhat disoriented at times. I was taken off guard by the depth of injuries that so many women suffer as they consider their own self-worth. A woman's image of the body-self, held up to familial and cultural expectations, often leads to a sense of not being worthy or good enough for the family or society that she lives within. A negative sense of self contributes to depression, and the number of women in the United States who suffer from depression is a sobering figure. The National Alliance on Mental Illness (NAMI) reports that an estimated one in eight women will face a major depression (2010). Depression affects self-evaluation. Negative self-evaluation, particularly when it takes on a body focus, contributes to the development of eating disorders. The Renfrew Center Foundation, a national nonprofit organization providing statistics regarding eating disorders, reports that "up to 1 in 5 women struggle with an eating disorder or disordered eating." Their website notes that "eating disorders have the highest mortality rate of any illness" (Renfrew Center Foundation for Eating Disorders, 2002). Eating disorders are complex illnesses that often respond to early intervention and treatment. This book promotes understanding and appreciation of the body-self to help women lift the weight of sadness that holds them, so they may navigate upon the waters and roadways of life. It contains art processes that may be used effectively in prevention and early intervention related to body image concerns, or which may complement the model of a multi-disciplinary approach to treatment of eating disorders.

PRINCIPLES AND METHODS USED IN THIS BOOK

The principles and methods used throughout the art processes in this book have a unified focus related to integration of the whole human being. Several theoretical models are explored and integrated around the theme of developing a healthy sense of body and self. Humanistic principles inherent in the human capacity for growth, recognition of worth and potential for self-fulfillment are practiced in the use of metaphors, symbols and stories. Existential and Gestalt principles that recognize the traveler's potential to experience herself as unique and whole are introduced and reinforced. Resistance is recognized as a natural response to the process, and travelers are able to navigate their life-vehicles into undiscovered territories at a pace that works for them. Troubled waters that surround the body-vessel are explored as internal and external factors that affect the overall function of the self. Emotions in response to beliefs about self and the world, environmental factors and relationships have the potential to stir the waters that rock the boat. Navigating through these waters and roadways is explored as a life process that begins early in life. Psychodynamic and object relations theories are relevant to the course of the journey starting at birth, and the traveler's ability to relate to self and others. Narrative therapy may be naturally incorporated in the art processes as travelers develop metaphors, symbols and images within storylines. Body image theory blends with all models utilized in this book, and expands on the cultural influences in the immediate environment, as well as those that lurk on the horizon. The practice of mindfulness, for the purpose of improving quality of life in the moment, steadies travelers on their voyage of self-discovery.

A METAPHORIC STORY

The following story reflects the use of symbols and metaphors to describe a traveler who has lost her way out on the waters of life:

A ship that appears to be disabled is tossed about on the water as a storm rages around her. The sails that usually help her stay on course, by shifting in a desired direction, hang helplessly, as if in a state of surrender. Dark clouds loom over the waters, and gusty winds whip up waves that pound the boat. Heavy rains pour down from the sky, as if in response to the sadness that fills the air. A woman sits inside of the boat, numbly taking in her surroundings; whatever she is able to see in the dark cabin. She knows that the boat's communication and directional equipment is no longer working, and she can't recall how long her ability to connect to the outside world has been shut down. She has lost faith in her vessel, and desperately longs for another ship to carry her through her journey. She has a strange sensation of being disconnected from her body, and she feels momentarily surprised by the relief that brings her. Operating from an innate sense of self-preservation, she overrides self-destructive feelings and launches a flare in a cry for help. She softly asks herself the question she knows she cannot answer, yet her acknowledgment of the unknown seems to bring some sense of comfort: "How did I get here, to this place in my life?"

The mood of the troubled waters surrounding the boat contributes to the emotional turmoil experienced by the traveler. Crashing waves that rock the vessel carry a lifetime of thoughts and feelings related to the self, particularly the body-self. She believes her body has committed mutiny in its revolt against her dreams and commands, yet she must continue along the waters of life, in the vessel that betrayed her. Her persistent, negative body evaluation keeps her trapped within a cycle such as Thompson, Heinburg, Altabe and Tantleff-Dunn's (1999) "hurricane effect." Williamson, Stewart, White and York-Crowe (2002) describe the "feedback loop" associated with the hurricane effect: "Because negative body images are likely to induce negative mood states such as anxiety and depression, the activation of negative mood can activate the body self-schema, resulting in the exacerbation of disturbed body image" (p.50). The traveler feels trapped, unable to free herself from the internal voice that sustains her skewed perception of reality.

Other boats have passed the woman by. Their failure to acknowledge her distress contributes to her despair. She does not feel validated or cared for, and she doubts her worthiness to experience either. She cannot see inside of the vessels that pass her. She is unaware that many of those ships traveling along the waters of life are having similar experiences, perhaps varying in duration and intensity. Numerous factors create extreme environmental conditions, resulting in ships that are disabled or in dry dock. The waterways and roadsides are filled with body-vehicles that are idling in doubt or despair. As a culture, we must ask ourselves the same question: "How did we get here, to this place?"

SELF-CONCEPT AT BIRTH

In order to gain greater understanding of our current condition, we go to the beginning of life when concept of self begins to form within the world of object relations. The developing sense of the body-self begins early in life, from the moment of birth, when contact with the primary caregivers begins. Krueger (2004) comments on the developing sense of self:

> *The close and careful attunement by the caretaker to all the sensory and motor contacts with the child forms the child's accurate and attuned self-container and foundation for the evolving psychological self. The caregiver's sensory-motor interaction with the infant's body, providing physical and psychological soothing for all the sensations and secure holding, occurs before there are words or language. (Krueger, 2004, p.31)*

Kravits (2008) points out the importance of attachment, particularly related to the child's developing internal world: "Attachment is a dyadic, emotion-regulating system that contributes to the development of internal representations of the self and the world" (p.140). She also explains the significance of secure attachment: "Secure attachment provides the individual with sufficient resources to be able to experience and explore the internal and external world congruently" (p.140). A child may respond to an attentive, nurturing provider by reflecting confidence and a standing in the world. A child may have difficulty bonding with a caregiver because of attachment style or caregiver behavior. Children who do not form meaningful bonds with others may question their own value in the world. Variations in attachment may directly affect body image. "Individuals who are insecure in attachment, whether due to self-perceived inadequacies or expectations of social rejections, may also be insecure about their physical worth and acceptability" (Cash and Fleming, 2004, p.282).

Krueger (2004) believes that self-awareness begins to manifest at 15–18 months of age, when a child "discovers himself or herself in the mirror and begins to say 'no.' This inaugurates the process whereby the infant experiences his or her differentiation. 'I am not an extension of you and your body and desire; this is where you end and I begin—my body is mine and mine alone'" (p.33).

A child may also assimilate the culture of body acceptance or rejection expressed by the primary caregiver, who is often the mother. Kearney-Cooke (2002) makes an astounding conclusion regarding the relevance of a mother's body image in relation to her developing child: "Today's young women are the first generation to be raised by mothers who typically reject their bodies and are often concerned about the size of their daughters' bodies from the moment of birth" (p.102). It is difficult to conceptualize this statement as anything other than a profound exaggeration; however, it seems to bear out when mothers speak honestly about their fears. Mothers commonly express concern that their daughters may not thrive in a culture that demands a specific standard of weight and beauty. Those fears are well founded in a mother's own life experiences, and the experiences of many (if not most) women that she knows.

SELF-CONCEPT AT SCHOOL AGE

When a child reaches school age, she is developing a sense of *being* in the world, as well as an awareness of other people's experience of being in the world. A child's self-reflective ability results in integration of the body-self, which in turn "contributes to affect and tension regulation, impulse control, self-monitoring, and the emergence of a sense of self-agency" (Krueger, 2004, p.31). She is influenced by an expanded world of object relations, and the cultural environment to a much broader extent. She is beginning to conceptualize self and the world around her, using concrete operations. Krueger (2004) writes that at the beginning of concrete operations "a definite sense of separation between self and object and a more distinct and accurate body image become possible as abstract ability crystallizes" (p.33). The way that children perceive themselves in the world continues to be influenced by parents and culture. In her work relating to children's developing perceptions of their own bodies, Linda Smolak

(2004) says that "parents can influence body image development by selecting and commenting on children's clothing, and appearance, or by requiring the child to look certain ways and to eat or avoid certain foods" (p.69).

Smolak also says that children are aware of the societal bias against fat people around the time they enter first grade. The message may be integrated into the developing sense of self: "Even in elementary school, overweight children report more body dissatisfaction and wish they were thinner" (p.68). Our culture's response to the growing concern for obesity among our child population has been to place the spotlight on kids who are overweight (by Western cultural standards). This has resulted in greater social rejection of those children. Some cultural messages, meant to be positive, may have a negative effect on self-esteem. For example, the popular television show *The Biggest Loser* is meant to inspire people to lose weight and become healthy; however, overweight kids integrate the concept of being fat, and being a *big loser*, into their personal schema. In this sense, the idea of weight as a measure of value is reinforced. Kids who are not overweight are affected by the cultural message of thinness. They live with the fear that they will become fat; therefore, less likeable and less valuable.

SELF-CONCEPT IN ADOLESCENCE

By the time a girl enters adolescence, her body may become the battleground in her struggle for a developing sense of identity. She will try on new relationships and experiences in a practice run for adulthood. She forms strong opinions on a wide variety of topics, and she feels an innate desire to be *heard* by others; her voice reflects her identity. Joan Borysenko (1996) describes cultural conditions that affect a teenage girl's ability to develop her voice: "We are socialized progressively to be nice, to please others, and not to ask embarrassing questions or raise difficult issues" (p.70). When an adolescent girl realizes that she cannot change the world around her, she moves towards that which she believes she *can* change. Her body becomes the focus of her attention; and her physical appearance becomes a kind of *visual voice* that the culture hears and responds to. Her confidence is strengthened by her sense of control over her body and appearance.

During the individuation process, an adolescent girl will likely seek an identity that differs from her mother's. When a mother is hyper-focused on maintaining a youthful body, her teen daughter may feel compelled to compete with that image to prove that she is also desirable and accepted in the world. Adolescence is also a time when significant changes in the body are taking place. "Pubertal development in girls is accompanied by an average weight gain of 50 pounds. This includes 20–30 pounds of fat, much of it deposited in the hips, thighs, buttocks, and waist. This normal biological process moves most girls from the dominant white ideal body shape" (Levine and Smolak, 2004, p.74).

The adolescent girl struggles to create her own, unique sense of identity in the world while maintaining a sense of belonging to her peer group. She is finding new ways to manage strong emotions as she faces the significant pressures and changes that are taking place.

SELF-CONCEPT IN ADULTHOOD

The desire for a particular body type during adolescence often carries into adulthood. Christine Northrup (1998), author of *Women's Bodies, Women's Wisdom*, says that most women have been "brainwashed" about what they should weigh. "So each of us in life, usually beginning in adolescence, moves through life with an ideal etched deeply in our brain" (p.692). That weight is often sought after, even after profound changes in the body, such as childbirth, have taken place. Women who struggle to maintain the same body as the one they had in high school may also engage in thoughts and behaviors that were a part of that period of life. When the body is not allowed to age in a healthy and graceful way, then the mind, body and spirit are forced to accommodate a *way of being* that does not fit. When a woman focuses on control over her body, she is distracted away from depth of relationships and experiences that occur. She is unable to move cognitively, emotionally and spiritually into the next stage of her life.

Women are conditioned to look either back in time to recall how their body appeared at a certain age, or forward in time to predict how their body may look in the process of aging. Because of this, women are losing quality of time in the moments they are living in. Anita Johnston (1996) says:

...only when we are in the here and the now can we really get filled up and be nourished by life. Life takes place only in the present. If you are obsessing about yesterday or planning for tomorrow, you will be unable to take in and receive whatever is in front of you that can be nourishing; a smile from a child, a compliment from a friend, the scent of a rose, a favorite tune, a brilliant sunset. (Johnston, 1996, p.33)

The practice of *mindfulness* helps women ground themselves in a non-judgemental attention to the experience in the present moment. Jon Kabat-Zinn (1993) describes the practice of becoming mindful for highly anxious people: "They're simply asked to observe, to be mindful, to stay in the body, and to watch what's going on in the mind, learning neither to reject things nor to pursue things, but just to let them be and let them go" (p.123). The traveler who is able to bring her attention to the moment that she is in, fully alive with her senses, will experience growth and renewal even in the midst of a terrible storm. She reconnects to the body-vessel that she travels within, and benefits from the awareness of the interconnectedness of her system as a whole: Kabat-Zinn reminds us that the mind and body are connected; they interact with each other, and they influence each other. If women are too busy, too discouraged or too sad to stay in the moment they are in, each moment becomes an opportunity to search for a better one. Mindfulness is practiced throughout the voyage of *self-discovery* in this book.

CULTURAL INFLUENCE
Cultural expectations are not necessarily conducive to the practice of mindfulness, because of the steady message that one must be working towards perfection. The messages that women receive via internet, television, theater, books and magazines create an ever-present anxiety based on a need to fix, change, or enhance appearance. Before a woman steps out of bed in the morning, she has likely spent some time wondering about what she will wear, what she will weigh, and how others will *see* her as she moves through the day. These thoughts may lead to other questions: "Will I be desired, respected or even accepted today?" The Western cultural demand for an ideal form of beauty has a tremendous impact on the first thoughts and feelings a woman experiences as she opens her eyes and greets the world. Somewhere

inside she knows that she has a short window of opportunity to *shine* in the world—before her body begins to visibly age and change. She considers ways to trick the effects of the biological time clock. Again, we must ask ourselves collectively, how did we get to this place?

Prior to the twenty-first century, as people in the United States conceptualized an exciting new era, there were so many things to look forward to in a rapidly changing time. Dreamers imagined a world with technology that would bring people closer together, increasing potential for exchange of ideas, problem solving, and overall advancements in human rights and conditions. Technology broadened outreach to world communities, promoting interaction with diverse peoples and cultures. In a curious parallel process, a collective fascination related to stereotypical and unrealistic beauty standards was becoming deeply embedded in the minds and lives of Western people. We "evolved" in such a way that women today face extraordinary pressure to meet beauty expectations determined by profit-driven corporations. As long as women believe they are not good enough, they will continue to buy products that they believe will help them achieve their goals. The bar for beauty has been set so high that even women who are considered beautiful by cultural standards do not think of themselves as beautiful. The expectations of beauty were established so they could never be met. In her book *The Beauty Myth*, Naomi Wolfe (2002) describes the current state of women:

> *More women have more money and power and scope and legal recognition than we have ever had before; but in terms of how we feel about ourselves physically, we may actually be worse off than our unliberated grandmothers. Recent research consistently shows that inside the majority of the West's controlled, attractive, successful working women, there is a secret "underlife" poisoning our freedom; infused with notions of beauty, it is a dark vein of self-hatred, physical obsessions, terror of aging, and dread of lost control. (Wolfe, 2002, p.10)*

In American culture, and the broader world community, women's bodies are objectified, and used as measurements of worth. The market is flooded with diet, beauty and fashion products that supposedly help women achieve a sense of being an accepted member of society. Kevin Richardson (2010) points to the prevalence of ads: "Not surprisingly over 75% of women's magazine covers include at least one message about how to change bodily appearance by diet, exercise or cosmetic surgery" (web page). The corporate sector profits from women's insecurities about themselves. It seems there are conveniently ignorant, possibly misogynistic men living in beautiful homes, driving luxurious cars, taking extraordinary vacations, because women hate their bodies. If company executives had to stand to account for manipulation of women for profit, then women of influence in the fashion and beauty industry would have to stand with men.

IN SEARCH OF THE IDEAL BODY:
THE DIET INDUSTRY

The multi-billion-dollar diet industry is an example of big business thriving on the culture of commercialized female beauty. Laura Cummings (2003) commented on the wealth of the diet industry at the turn of the twenty-first century: "There are no official statistics for spending on diet products, but estimates vary from 40 billion dollars to 60 billion dollars in the US alone—more than the combined value of the government's budget for health, education, and welfare" (web page). Carolyn Costin (2007), a specialist in the field of eating disorders, says, "Being a female in America seems synonymous with being on a diet, and the dieting has become more severe and more entrenched, starting at younger ages" (p.23). Women typically respond to diets that don't work by abandoning them and moving on to another. The industry is thriving on women's failed diet attempts and the provoked desire to maintain or sustain the ideal body type.

The "ideal" body sought by Western women is strongly influenced by the fashion industry. The obviously emaciated bodies may no longer be an exception to the ideal standard of beauty. Women may engage in excessive exercise, practice compensatory behaviors such as laxative abuse and purging, and participate in diets, as they work towards achieving this very specific body type. Fashion models risk physical and emotional health problems attempting to keep their bodies under control. Johann Hari (2009), an award-winning British journalist, questions how we react to the world of fashion: "When did our collective disgust at the sickness and sicked-up stomach juices that fuel the fashion industry get replaced by the oh-so-ironic appreciation? When did even most liberals and feminists stop snubbing it and start wrestling their way to the rope-line in search of a goody bag?" (web page). Western women seek out services to change what dieting cannot. Procedures such as breast implants, breast reductions, "butt implants," liposuction, botox and face-lifts have become almost commonplace in the culture, particularly for women who live or work in parts of the country where physical appearance or obvious aging may be a barrier to employment. Hollywood may lead the nation in determining the overall value of women based on age and physical appearance.

IMAGES ALONG THE WAY

As women travel along the waters and roadways of life, they see billboards or cultural messages with images that contribute to the depreciation of self. Naomi Wolfe (2002) reminds travelers that they can empower themselves in the presence of harmful images: "While we cannot directly affect the images, we can drain them of their power. We can turn away from them, look directly at one another, and find alternative images of beauty in the female subculture" (p.277). Female activist Susie Orbach (2007) believes that we should expand relatable images: "We need to broaden the images of girls so that they can identify themselves in the world of images they live in" (front page of blog). Throughout the art processes in this book, women navigate their body-vessels away from what is directed by the culture, to celebrate diversity and uniqueness of self in body, mind and spirit.

THE GUIDE'S ROLE IN SELF-DISCOVERY NAVIGATION

The story of the woman stranded in her vessel out on the waters of life continues as a relief boat, carrying a guide (facilitator), arrives to offer aid to the weary traveler. The guide is female; however, the information provided for guides throughout the book is meant for all facilitators. The guide's first responsibility is to help the distressed traveler regain basic operation of her ship. She seeks balance in her initial intervention as she delivers ideas and information related to potential physical and mental safety concerns, while instilling a sense of empowerment and hope for the future. Hope will lift the sails of the ship, allowing her to move forward again. The guide travels with the woman on her journey of self-discovery via the world of creative expression and connection to others. She will stand with her as she moves through the landscapes of the imagination, to explore the world of self that exists beneath the skin. As women prepare to set out on the journey of self-discovery, their guides pause to consider maps, logs and opinions of those who have helped to plot courses for other travelers. This information will assist guides in exploring the known passageways, and planning for obstacles that may lie ahead.

BUILDING TRUST

The woman on her boat experiences numbing sensations—a life preserver that has helped her to maintain physical life in the midst of a tumultuous storm. Through the experientials, she will learn that her thoughts and emotions can be safely identified, expressed and managed in the context of a validating environment. Hass-Cohen (2008) says:

> The support and skills of an attuned art therapist helps recruit, express and hold the relational self in mind while allowing for the expression of needed emotions and motivations. The realization of emotions in artwork becomes a natural accompaniment to completing higher cortical tasks. Emotions such as frustration and joy, which emerge in the artwork, are experienced whilst learning to trust another person, in our case, the art therapist. (Hass-Cohen, 2008, p.39)

The female guide may face significant challenges in building trust, as a result of cultural influences that the woman has been exposed to. Throughout her travels, she has experienced subtle and obvious messages relating to how women interact with each other. Some of those messages and experiences have been positive. Others have left her fearful and lacking trust in other women. Until a sense of safety is established, an unfamiliar female guide may be perceived like the "unknown woman" described by Naomi Wolfe (2002): "The unknown woman, the myth would like women to believe, is unapproachable; under suspicion before she opens her mouth because she is Another Woman, and beauty thinking urges women to approach one another as possible adversaries until they know they are friends" (p.75). Once trust is established, the guide will assess the traveler's willingness and ability to work with other women if she plans to join the group of ships who have gathered out on the waters of life.

The relationship between the traveler and her guide helps to create the safe environment where images are created, and feelings are processed. The female guide must maintain an awareness of possible perceptions and projections of the traveler. Gillespie (1994) describes the relationship between the traveler and the art therapist when she says, "Art therapy partakes to an unusually great extent the kind of affective interactions that were part of the early mother–child experience" (p.4). She also reminds us of the space that the guide works within that holds ongoing, dynamic object relations: "The effective therapist is comfortable in that shared play space, not the physical space in which the art activities occur, but in a shared, subjective world space that in later life retains the mutuality of the early mother and child relationship" (p.4).

From the moment of initial contact, the guide begins the process of building trust by actively listening to the woman's concerns regarding her situation, particularly her thoughts and feelings about the body-vessel that she travels within. The guide sits at her level, makes eye contact, and mirrors back the cognitive and emotional experience described and expressed by the traveler. She establishes her qualifications as a guide by sharing some information about background and training, as well as her experience in traveling with other women on the waters and roads of life. It is imperative that the guide has explored feelings related to her own body image. This is an ongoing process that can initiate strong emotional responses. If the guide has not explored the vessel she travels within, she may become lost out on the waters and roads.

The art processes move travelers to the core of self-evaluation, and relationships with others in the world that contribute to that evaluation. A male guide addresses any doubts that women may have when working with a person of the opposite gender. He acknowledges limitations in relating to the traveler as female because he has traveled his journey in a vehicle that differs from her own. However, he stresses the strengths that he brings as an interested and caring observer of the female experience. He highlights his ability to relate to the woman traveler as one human being to another.

There are many others who share the traveler's experience: The National Centre for Eating Disorders (2009) states that "obsessive concern about body shape and weight has become so common among western women of all ages that it is now the norm. Moreover, results of a large survey indicate that body image problems are more common in the USA than any other nation." Sarah Grogan (2008) addresses the expansion of body image studies that also include older women. She explains that body image may be looked at as a "multifaceted construct that includes more than weight and shape concern" (preface). A woman's sense of her body affects all aspects of the life experience; she becomes bound to the established and reinforced negative self-schemas. On the extended voyage of self-discovery, women explore their own value and definition beyond outward appearance. The traveler is supported by the guide, and perhaps fellow travelers, in looking *upon* her vessel, *within* her vessel and *beyond* her vessel. To do this, an environment of trust must be established.

PREPARING FOR THE JOURNEY

Every participant involved in the body image processes described in this book should meet with their guide before embarking on the voyage of self-discovery. The facilitator knows that travelers may have had extended time wandering, or lost, out on the waters and roadways of life. She assesses for any intent the traveler may have to harm or destroy her life vessel (self) before inviting her to join the group of ships that have gathered for the journey. The art processes in this book move the traveler below the surface of conscious awareness, to undefended territories of the body-self awareness. The information derived from these processes is likely to *stir the waters* surrounding the boats, and may cause some instability before steadiness is obtained. Guides should assess for travelers' abilities to develop positive coping strategies that will help identify and manage emotional responses before, during and after the experientials. Participants commonly report anxiety in anticipation of the art exercises, and a variety of emotions may occur during the processes. The guide reassures the traveler that she will learn new ways to manage those emotions as she continues her journey of self-discovery. If the guide determines that the traveler is not ready for the voyage with other vessels (group members), she will refer her to another guide who will meet with her individually to help her prepare for such a journey. From the very beginning, the guide instills hope that the art processes themselves help women who have become lost in a storm, within a body-vessel that is no longer valued or trusted. Figure 1.1 shows a sample workshop flyer.

Art & Mindfulness

An experiential ⚓ workshop exploring the use of 🖌 Art to enhance Mindfulness.

Presented By:
Margaret Hunter,
M.A., ATR
Registered Art Therapist

No previous art experience necessary.

Wear comfortable clothing.

Saturday,
July 9, 2011
9:00 am - 2:30 pm

1311 E Street
Modesto, CA
95354
209-575-3324

Cost:
Includes lunch

Create a boat to symbolize internal and external qualities of self.
Take a metaphoric voyage upon the waters of life.

Figure 1.1 "Art & Mindfulness" flyer

RESISTING THE CALL TO ADVENTURE

When looking out to the horizon, travelers have some sense of what lies ahead in the immediate future. All that exists beyond the horizon, out in the distance and beneath the waters and ground, remains a mystery. Guides move forward knowing that travelers fear the unknown; therefore, there is often resistance to the journey. As a traveler seeks to understand her life in a profound and meaningful way, she must face whatever lies within the shadows, and below the surfaces of the waters and land. The woman who lost her way out on the waters of life somehow found strength to reach outside of herself to ask for help. Now she must find courage to travel into the unknown realms of her internal world. In her book *Eating in the Light of the Moon*, Anita Johnston (1996) describes a descent into the underworld in search of strength: "For the longest time she has been frightened of this journey into the darkness, frightened of what horrors she may find there, and she has dealt with her fear by trying to avoid it, by denying the importance of the dark places of her being where her deepest secrets reside" (p.131). The guide reminds the traveler of Johnston's message regarding the power of such a journey: "In the darkness, she is reborn. Her shadow sister with the power to destroy also holds the power of transformation and renewal" (p.135). The traveler explores parts of self in a world that exists beneath the skin. She shines the light in places that have been ignored, forgotten or rejected. In this process, the guide and fellow travelers help her to acknowledge herself as a whole human being with strengths and weaknesses, imperfections and beauty. She discovers, or rediscovers, herself with the eyes of an artist. In the process, she also begins to understand how she became so lost along the way.

USE OF ART TO FACILITATE GROWTH

The journey of self-discovery begins with a story conveyed in the language of metaphors; a form of expression woven into the art processes. Krueger (2004), a psychodynamic theorist, describes the image of the body in the interplay of the mind, within the realms of the imagination:

> *The body appears in the narrative of dreams, metaphors and symptoms as a symbolic vision of inner landscapes, mysterious structures and*

configurations, and geographical terrain. An idea as well as a fact, the body is a container of emotional experience, and the body image is a Rorschach onto which fantasies, meaning and significance are projected. The body self and image are ideas, like that of the ego; the body is a fact. The body self and its image are created by, and live within, the imagination, the map within the actual territory of the body. (Krueger, 2004, p.30)

The use of art to facilitate growth and healing is the focus of each art experience throughout this book. The processes may be done individually, or with a group of travelers. Cathy Malchiodi (2007) describes art therapy: "Art therapy is essentially the marriage of two disciplines: art and psychology. Aspects of the visual arts, the creative process, human development, among others, are important to the definition and scope of art therapy" (p.3). Malchiodi also says that "the emphasis is generally first on developing and expressing images that come from inside the person, rather than those he or she sees in the outside world" (p.4). Images produced by travelers become *mirrors* that reflect back aspects of the self that exist beneath the surface of the skin. The images also provide valuable information concerning the traveler's connection to the world around her. Hass-Cohen (2008) says, "In the art therapist's presence, the artwork is an expression of how the self organizes internally as well as relationships with others. It is a visual reiteration of the interplay between the person and their environment" (p.21). The expressive art space may be viewed as multi-cultural in nature: the traveler joins into the culture of the art experience, and travels within the foreign land of positive self-evaluation. The guide introduces the traveler to the culture (of self-appreciation) in the language of art: "The language of the arts, with their metaphors, symbols, rituals, and play, are all essential to our comprehension of the world and our overall well-being as individuals and as a larger community. The languages of the arts resonate deep within our being" (Schnetz, 2005, p.36).

TOOLS AND SURVIVAL GEAR: USE OF
THEORY TO ASSIST TRAVELERS

The securely anchored and experienced guide carries a storage locker containing a variety of tools and survival gear. Every storage locker is unique because of what the guide carries with her. The guide assisting women on the voyage of self-discovery may pull tools from various approaches and theoretical models of which she holds knowledge and experience. If one form of intervention does not work, the guide may selectively try another. Harriet Wadeson (1987), an eclectic art therapist, stresses the importance of knowing *why* a particular approach is being used. She says, "Theory is an essential part of our work" (p.306). The storage locker, when opened, looks similar to the colorful and diverse art materials in the room. The guide must also be familiar with the materials and know how to use them. Moon (2002) reminds us: "The art therapist, irrespective of theoretical approach, target population, or practice setting, wields enormous influence over the nature of the therapeutic encounter simply by deciding what materials to provide to clients and how to guide clients in using those materials" (p.50). The variety of art materials complements the multi-sensory experience of being fully present and alive. The colors, textures and shapes of the materials that are used blend together to create beautiful stories with illustrations. A suggested list of art materials is provided below:

- White butcher (poster) paper (36" paper roll)
- Pencils and erasers, pens
- Paints (acrylic and/or tempura)
- Paint palettes
- Water container (to dip paint brushes, and clean paint brushes)
- Watercolor paint trays
- Brushes
- Markers
- Colored pencils
- Soft pastels
- Oil pastels
- Strings, ribbons
- Glitter and/or glitter glue (glitter glue is less messy)
- Glue

- Warm glue gun

- Beads

- Shells

- Colored tissue paper

- Cloth

- Cards

- Magazines

- Masking tape

- White drawing paper, different sizes (9" × 12" (22 × 30cm); 11" × 14" (28 × 35cm); and 14" × 17" (35 × 43cm); and 18" × 24" (46 × 61cm)).

The guide may use a narrative (storytelling) approach as she journeys with travelers into the stories of their lives. She helps travelers recognize their strengths and abilities, and encourages development of supportive relationships. This connection with others helps the traveler overcome problems so that the desired life story is achieved. The guide helps travelers see obstacles from different points of view, so that alternative outcomes may be explored and developed. Travelers externalize their problems out loud, contemplating different solutions. The stories are expressed through the art experience, and the telling of the stories. The traveler gains strength by looking at current narratives with curiosity and creativity. She takes pen and art materials in hand as she becomes the author of her own life journey. Eventually, she will learn to define herself beyond the body-vehicle that she travels within. She will carry her stories and images with her throughout the remainder of her real-life adventure.

Gestalt therapy naturally complements the art experiences in this book. All travelers, regardless of their experience with art and creativity, are invited to join in the process of artistic expression. Many travelers initially report their belief that "art" belongs to the world of artists, collectors and patrons. This is a world that perhaps they have traveled through, but have not stopped to visit on an intimate level. Korb, Davenport and Korb (1996) say:

From a holistic Gestalt perspective, creativity is not the province of "the Arts," artists, or any select stratum of society or discipline. Nor is it an achievement. It must ultimately be embraced as a birthright and an existential constant; whether we learn to use it consciously, responsibly, and proactively or not. The active word is awareness. *(Korb, Davenport and Korb, 1996, web page)*

The facilitator pays attention to the creative process of each participant as they move towards self-awareness and growth. Travelers give voice to the meaning of their art, as well as to the process of making it.

The relaxation and guided imagery exercises throughout the book enhance the art processes, and highlight the importance of the mind-and-body connection. The traveler is encouraged to experience her thoughts and feelings within her body, in the context of the creative process.

SUMMARY

Guides are encouraged to bring their own theoretical approaches to the art processes in this book. I encourage you to practice ahead of time so that you are able to "feel" yourself fully present in the approach you bring to the table. Guides should have some knowledge of the waterways and roads that lie ahead, before embarking on a journey with others. The journey of self-discovery is life changing. Travelers become aware of the amazing qualities of self that lie beneath the skin. They develop a deeper appreciation for the body-vehicle that takes each one of us through this incredible life journey.

2

Lessons from the Ocean

Riding the Waves of Emotions

INTRODUCTION

Women take many journeys throughout their lifetimes. Adventures may include external trips, which involve physical movement from one place to another, and internal imaginary expeditions, which occur during dream states and periods of creativity. A woman's mind and body work together as she moves through the physical world, as well as the odyssey of her imagination and unconscious mind. All journeys, real and imagined, require participation from the physical body, the mind and the part of self that emotes and creates. Women incorporate all of these aspects of self as they prepare for, and fulfill, their journeys. As a woman develops a greater awareness of her mind–body connection, she moves forward with hope, strength and confidence that she will be able to face whatever lies ahead on the waters and roadways of life.

Ideas for physical trips that a woman takes in her lifetime may originate from information gathered from a variety of sources. Women frequently consult with friends, travel agents and online sites as they consider places to visit. A woman's mind moves her body into activity that will help her achieve whatever is needed before, during and after each trip. She shops; packs; boards planes and other modes of transportation; carries luggage; walks, runs and hikes. Her sense of excitement throughout the journey process may eclipse changes occurring in her body related to reduced sleep, shifts in food intake, increased muscle activity and prolonged periods of concentration. The mind, with its amazing capacity for dreaming and planning, may lose or lack connection to the body-vehicle that carries the woman through her life journeys. She may inadvertently set out upon her adventure in a depleted system, with diminished resistance to physical ailments and emotional stress. As she learns to listen to, and understand, the language of her body, she is able to move her system into harmony, improving the overall quality of her life experiences.

A woman may be so preoccupied when planning for real-life journeys that she is not mindful of the places she is able to travel within the expansive frontiers of her mind, imagination and storylines. She may lose sight of the benefits of traveling to places near and far during periods of daydreaming, when her weary mind moves to escape responsibilities and worries. Once a woman drifts into the world of daydreaming, she is likely to force herself back to conscious thought, resisting her own needs and desires to experience even short periods of fantasy, pleasure and well-being. When we do allow ourselves to shift into the realm of the imagination, we become inspired and motivated to create; we are able to paint images upon the canvases of our minds. The journeys we are able to take during periods of daydreaming may be extraordinary in nature, even surpassing the experiences of real-life travels.

Journeys may also have origins in the conceptualization of dreams, or the development of unconscious desires that surface. The incredible world of dreams that we experience when we are asleep also provides opportunities for travel; we move back and forth in time to places we have been, places we would like to go, and fantastic places that only exist in the world of our unconscious mind. Once awakened from the dream state, we may experience residual, multi-sensory recall of the places we visited, the people we saw or interacted with, the problems we encountered, and the emotions that we felt. The sights, sounds, tastes, smells and things that we touch throughout the day may seem curiously familiar, taking us back to our dream experience. A woman may design an actual trip based on vivid images of foreign people and lands she encountered in her dreams. Once awakened from a dream journey, a woman may long for adventure and may plan a trip to fulfill that need.

It is during the busiest moments of trip preparation and follow-through that women may benefit most from relaxation and guided imagery. This practice brings awareness back to internal signals, promoting connection between mind and body. Breath awareness is a simple, yet powerful, technique that serves as a foundation for the relaxation process. Breath sustains life; the awareness of breath flowing through the system enhances physical and mental well-being. During the guided imagery process, the ocean is presented as a metaphor to reinforce the experience of flow, movement and rhythm. Women begin relaxation and guided imagery by sitting or lying down with backs as straight as possible to allow air flow throughout the body. They inhale, and imagine warm energy moving throughout their bodies—an energy that calms the system and facilitates movement of stress and tension away from the body. Women are guided into an awareness of their own tempo of breathing, like the steady and soothing rhythm of ocean waves.

The word *inspiration* is used to describe the act of taking air into the lungs. Merriam-Webster's Online Dictionary (2012) offers alternate meanings for this word: inspiration is described as "The quality of being inspired." Artists may experience inspiration as a process of taking in thoughts, emotions and sensations, and then allowing them to flow through the mind, body and spirit. When an artist becomes interested in, or affected by, something within the physical world or spiritual realm, she moves that perception or sensation to the internal world of cognition and imagination where an image is created and expressed outside of the body. To become aware of breath is to be alive; to become inspired is to experience that life more completely. Merriam-Webster's Online Dictionary (2012) also defines inspiration as "The action or power of moving the intellect or emotions." As women become aware of their breathing, they acknowledge thoughts and feelings that move through the mind and body, like waves of the ocean moving onto the shore. In the guided imagery process, images that are brought into conscious awareness may be inspired by the words of the facilitator: memories of past experiences and dreams of what could be. Those images are acknowledged, and moved into the realm of the imagination, where they are used in the creative process.

Workshops are almost always attended by women with a wide variety of experience with relaxation and guided imagery. Women who have taken yoga classes often express familiarity and comfort in the practice of breath awareness and focus on the mind–body connection. Some participants have taken part in exercise classes that incorporate breath awareness in relation to cardio fitness. There are usually few women in this first group who have experienced a blend of relaxation, guided imagery and creative expression. It is not unusual for women to develop some hesitation or fear of the unknown, as expressed in verbal and nonverbal resistance to the process. The guide remains in tune to whatever is taking place in the room and responds with understanding and encouragement. This first experiential introduces the practice of mindfulness, which brings women to a non-judgemental experience of self in the here and now. The guide explains that this is the starting place on the journey of self-discovery. Travelers will learn skills to manage thoughts and emotions that are experienced throughout the life journey.

In this chapter, travelers take time to relax and rest for awhile before moving forward on their journey. Once participants have practiced breath awareness and muscle relaxation, they are guided into the world of the imagination where the ocean, as a representation of self, comes to life through an imaginative, multi-sensory experience. As members move through the guided imagery process, picturing themselves standing near the ocean, they are encouraged to acknowledge any sense of vulnerability that may arise. The guide reassures travelers that they are safe, and able to choose images that they would like to develop and explore. Again, thoughts, feelings and sensations are acknowledged and allowed to move through the mind and body. As each woman imagines herself standing on the shore of the ocean, she becomes attuned to the rhythm of the sea and begins to experience emotional and physical regulation. Her body, mind and spirit rest. She continues to breathe warm energy into her body, while allowing images to enter her mind. She imagines the scene before her, considering the sights, sounds, smells, tastes and sensations that she encounters. Should she become uneasy during the process, she may return to any image or memory that helps her to feel safe and comforted. Women develop a greater sense of mastery in their ability to move through any life experiences using skills to help manage distressing thoughts, feelings and/or sensations.

The multi-sensory experience of the ocean facilitates awareness of movement, change and transition. The guide reminds travelers that small transitions, as well as larger ones, often present opportunities for transformation. During the guided imagery process, women are transitioned from the world of wakefulness to a dream-like state where images are developed and incorporated into body, mind and spirit. These mental images are transformed into external drawings in the creative process. The guide provides the directive to "draw a picture of your multi-sensory experience with the ocean." The multi-sensory memories of the moments spent on the ocean shore help to bring the drawings to life. Very diverse, and personal, experiences of the ocean take form in the drawings; these representations reflect each woman's relationship with the ocean-self.

Women move into a circle for group discussion with their fellow travelers. This is an important aspect of the workshop because women are meeting for the first time to verbalize thoughts and feelings in the presence of other women. Women talk about self in the language of creativity; they find themselves in the ocean waves and in the life above and beneath the surface of the water. They are the boats and rocks; the dolphins and mermaids. They find their moods in places like the sun and clouds, and in the intensity of the waves pushing onto shore. They explore their relationships as they view the way that images in the drawing interact with each other. Every woman's perspective is unique; she is the only one who stands in her body, on the shore of the ocean.

Each artist is asked if she is open to comments from her fellow group members. Participants are encouraged to be mindful of their comments, keeping them in a first-person point of view, with caution regarding the superimposition of thoughts and feelings over those of the artist's. The guide observes the process, and provides direction and support when necessary. Not all women will be open to comments from others during the first group processing session. Participants are in a state of transition, moving towards transformation on the voyage of self-discovery; allowing self to be vulnerable in the presence of others occurs like a developmental milestone that takes place when the traveler is ready. As each traveler looks upon her drawing of the ocean, she senses that her maiden voyage out upon the waters of life is about to begin. She gathers skills she has learned in this first process, places them in her imagined backpack, and sets out to build a boat for her journey.

EXPERIENTIAL

Theme

The following relaxation and guided imagery process capitalizes on our mind's ability to create positive, multi-sensory experiences. During this exercise, participants practice relaxation before entering an awake, dreamlike state where the imagination is guided to a multi-sensory experience involving images of the ocean. Women take a journey by sea, to the world of the imagination; they are immersed in the culture and language of metaphors.

Metaphors

> Women naturally identify with the ocean because of some obvious shared qualities: the timeless beauty that inspires poets, musicians and artists; existence of forceful energy that lies beneath the surface; the ability to soothe, the capacity to nurture, the containment of water and cellular life within both bodies; unspoken emotional qualities such as moodiness, restlessness, anger and joy; and the ability to be adaptive. All are constant forces that are necessary for human survival.

Objectives

> We will focus on breath awareness, muscle relaxation and stress energy release from the body. Next, we will develop a multi-sensory connection with the ocean as we practice *being fully present* in the moment, acknowledging thoughts and feelings that come and go. We allow release of stress and tension that is carried within the body.
>
> This exercise will increase awareness of moment-to-moment transitions as we acknowledge the *shift* to the world of imagery and artistic engagement in a drawing process.

Settings

RELAXATION AND GUIDED IMAGERY

Participants will need room to sit or lie down. Offer a choice of chairs and mats if possible. Use low or adjusted lighting as desired. Place a bowl containing sand and shells in a visible place for all to see. If you have concerns regarding interruptions, place a "Do not disturb" sign on the door. Participants will need a table or flat surface to work on their drawings. Some type of music player is required if you decide to incorporate music in the process.

ART PROCESS

- Music: A CD that blends the sound of instruments with ocean waves. Use for the relaxation and guided imagery exercise as well as the art process.

- Art materials: White paper. Standard-size paper works fine. Colored pencils or markers.

DIALOGUE AND REFLECTION

In an ideal setting, chairs or mats are set up in a circular setting to promote a sense of connection amongst participants.

Relaxation and Guided Imagery Process

[Read out loud slowly, allowing pauses between sentences.]

Sit or lie in a comfortable position. If you are sitting, make sure your back and neck are straight, yet comfortable. Close your eyes and place your hands on your stomach. If you are not comfortable closing your eyes, then focus on the bowl of sand and shells [that has been placed in a visible position in the room].

Begin to notice your breathing moving in and out of your body. [pause] Feel your breath moving down into your abdomen. As you breathe in, you should feel your stomach expanding outward. Breathe in, pause for a moment, then exhale. [pause] As you exhale, breathe out as much air as possible. [longer pause] Feel your breathing falling in sync with the rhythm of the ocean waves that you hear.

Now, imagine that you are inhaling warm energy into your body. [pause] As you breathe in slowly, feel the warm energy entering your body. As you breathe out, feel the stress and tension that you carry move out of your body, and away from you. [longer pause]

We will start by focusing attention on the feet. You feel your awareness shifting to your feet, and your toes. [longer pause] Gently wiggle the toes on your feet. You feel all of the muscles in your toes and feet relax as you breathe in energy that moves down your body, into your feet. [longer pause] Now, feel yourself breathing away tension that is held there. In this moment, you do not have a need to use your feet…they can be totally at rest, filled with warm energy. [longer pause]

Move your focus upwards, to your calves. Feel the muscles in your calves relaxing, filling with warm energy as you breathe in. [longer pause]. As you exhale, you are releasing all of the tension that you carry there. Your calves feel light, and warmed by the energy that you breathe in.

Continue to move upward in your body. Feel the muscles in your thighs, hips and bottom relaxing. [longer pause] Remember to pay attention to the air that you breathe in, the warm energy that creates a sense of warmth and lightness. As you breathe out, feel yourself breathing away all of the tension that you carry in your lower body. Feel yourself at rest. [longer pause]

Continuing to move upward in your body, feel the muscles in your lower back relaxing. Breathe in warm energy [longer pause]…and breathe away all of the tension that you hold in your lower back. Pay attention to your stomach for a moment, a place where worry and stress are often held. Focus on your breath moving into your stomach, filling it with warm energy. [longer pause] As you exhale, you breathe away all of the stress and tension that you hold in your stomach. Your stomach feels peaceful…at rest. [longer pause]

Now focus your awareness on your chest and upper back. [longer pause] Another place where we hold much of our worry and stress. Focus on your breathing…breathe in warm energy to your chest and upper back. [pause] Feel your muscles relax as you become lighter, and filled with warmth. You feel your breath move out of your body, carrying all of the stress and tension that you carry there. [longer pause]

Become aware of your shoulders, a place where we may carry the weight of the world. Breathe in, allowing the muscles to relax and fill with warm energy. [pause] Allow all of your worries and stress to move away from your shoulders as you breathe out. [longer pause] Move down your arms, towards your elbows, and wrists, your hands and fingers. [pause] Feel all of the muscles in your arms relaxing as you breathe in warm energy. [longer pause] Wiggle your fingers, as you breathe in warm, creative energy. [longer pause] Your fingers are alive with creative energy, ready to do the work of the imagination. [longer pause]

Move back up the arms, towards the elbows, and the shoulders. You feel light, and relaxed. [pause] Focus your attention on your neck, the part of self that connects the mind and the body. Breathe in warm energy, and send it gently to your neck. [longer pause] Move upwards, into your face. Begin to relax all of the muscles in your face…your cheeks, your eyes, your forehead. [longer pause] Continue to feel yourself breathing in warm energy that relaxes your face [longer pause] and your head. [longer pause]

You are relaxed, and alive with warm energy. You can now open the doors to the imagination, a place inside of you that is filled with gentle, creative energy. The warm, creative energy is released into your body [longer pause] and it moves down into your fingertips. You begin the practice of *being like the ocean*. You are fully present in the moment; there is no need to think about the past, or what is yet to come. You are fully present in your body, in this room, in this moment.

Let your thoughts and feelings move through your body, losing momentum as they travel…like the ocean tides that rise and then diminish as they move onto shore. If you are holding any thoughts or feelings in your mind or body, acknowledge their presence, then feel them move away in the gentle rhythm of the waves.

Imagine that you are standing near the ocean…watching…listening to the waves. You feel the connection of the rhythm of the ocean to the rhythm of your body. You hear the pulse of the waves washing onto shore… You feel your heart beating. [pause]

Acknowledge any sense of vulnerability you may feel standing near the ocean. You are an observer of your environment. You choose whatever you would like to see, hear, smell, taste and touch. You are completely safe…warm and relaxed. Remember that at any time you may return to an image that feels safe and comforting. [longer pause]

Look out to the ocean… What do you see? [longer pause] Look at the colors in the water… Watch how they change. Are the colors affected by the light, or shadows? Do you see the movement of the waves? Do you see anything inside of the water…or outside of the water? [longer pause] Do you see sand or rocks close to the water? [longer pause] What else do you see? [pause]

What do you hear, standing near the ocean? [longer pause] Notice the sound of the water…does the intensity change? [longer pause] What else do you hear? [longer pause]

As you stand near the ocean, what do you smell? [longer pause] Are the odors strong, or subtle? Are they constant, or do they shift like the tides? [longer pause]

Is there anything that you taste, or could taste, standing near the ocean? [longer pause] Would the taste be bitter, sweet, sour or salty? [longer pause] Are the tastes foreign or familiar?

What can you touch, as you stand near the ocean? [longer pause] If you would like, imagine yourself reaching down to touch the water. How does it feel? [longer pause] Can you feel the sand around you? What is the texture of the sand on your feet? You may reach down to touch the sand if you would like. Is there anything else you see around you that you would like to touch, or hold? [longer pause]

Spend a few moments in this place, feeling safe, relaxed and fully alive with all of your senses. [long pause]

When you are ready, become present in the room and open your eyes. Stretch if you would like.

[Allow a few moments for everyone to become present in the room.]

Art Process

The ocean in its steadiness and constancy is also ever in motion, ever changing. The changes that occur in our lives are sometimes referred to as *transitions*. If we took time to look back on our life journeys, we would likely recall transitions that caused significant change or upheaval. The impact of the seemingly insignificant shifts that occur on a regular basis is not so obvious. These smaller transitions, however, are the building blocks for transformations to take place.

Each morning we experience transition and transformation as we move from a sleep state, to an awake state. We transition from the world of dreams to the world of consciousness and the real world around us. The creative problem solving and healing that we are able to do during sleep carries over in the transition and we are transformed by a new awareness of our life experience.

You are transitioning from the world of guided imagery and a multi-sensory connection with the ocean, to the physical world and the realm of creativity. Residual sensations from the guided imagery process will carry over into representations of the ocean in relation to self; your ocean self.

As you sit quietly, listening to the music and the waves, go back to the moment when you were standing near the ocean. [pause] Remember things you observed; the sounds you heard; the smells and tastes you experienced; and the things that you imagined touching at the ocean shore. These sensory memories will help you to bring dimension and life to your very personal drawing of your experience of the ocean. Using pencils or markers, draw a picture of your multi-sensory experience with the ocean.

Dialogue and Reflection Process

Possible topics for discussion:

- Can you share your image? If it had a voice, what might it say?

- Was there a part of this experience that you want to explore more or learn more about?

- What role did your thoughts and feelings play in the process?

- Describe the initial experience of standing near the ocean. Address any sense of vulnerability... Did you feel safe? Peaceful?

- How are you interacting with the ocean?

- Were there any physical, spiritual or emotional qualities of the ocean that you identified with?

- Are you in your drawing? If so, how are you represented?

- Is there anything that "stood out" in the multi-sensory process?

- What is the overall mood of your drawing?

- Did you have any thoughts or feelings not related to the process, during the process?

- Were you able to acknowledge these thoughts and feelings without judgement?

- Were you able to allow the thoughts and feelings to move through you and dissipate like the waves of the ocean?

Homework

You have been provided with an envelope to hold your drawing of the ocean. The envelope will protect your artwork as you leave here, to continue your journey on the waters of life. One must internalize the contents of the envelope to hold the transformation that occurred in the relaxation and guided imagery process today. That transformation continues as you move along on your journey.

Place your drawing in a visible place and bring your multi-sensory awareness of the ocean to your conscious mind to experience, whenever you would like. Continue to practice the breathing and relaxation techniques, while finding the place within you where this transformation lives.

Lessons from the Ocean

Artist's Statement

During the guided imagery I could almost feel the cold water running across my feet, while my toes sank down into the sand. I saw an amazing rock out in the water. It gave me a sense of being "grounded." I wondered if I could find that feeling inside of myself.

I felt a sense of fear because of the strong waves, but somehow I also felt calm and at peace because I knew I was safe, and the waves couldn't hurt me. I know my feelings can't hurt me. Like Margaret said, they will come in, and move away. I love the sea. I am trying to love myself.

Figure 2.1 Embrace the sea

Figure 2.2 Feeling my senses

Figure 2.3 Only one bite missing

3

Art and Mindfulness

The Maiden Voyage Upon the Waters of Life

INTRODUCTION

Travelers continue their journey and prepare to move forward upon the open seas. They have been introduced to the ocean as a representation of self, a metaphor which continues to evolve in this chapter. Now, the ocean takes on an expansive meaning, symbolizing the *waters of life*, and all that is held within the waters. Participants continue to develop skills that will help manage whatever lies ahead on their journeys. They begin by creating a vessel to travel within as they set sail upon the waters. Working with a wide variety of art materials, each woman develops a boat to represent qualities of self, including body, mind and spirit. Women also design anchors to accompany the boats on their journeys. Anchors provide stability during heavy storms; they help travelers feel *grounded* even though land may be far from sight. During this experiential, women work individually, and then in small groups, to create metaphoric representations of the waters of life. Women offer validation and support to fellow travelers as they witness the launch of each boat on its maiden voyage.

Throughout this book, identifiable objects are used in the art processes to help facilitate the creative exploration of self. When a woman looks into a mirror, she views herself with critical eyes. She may become distracted, or fixated on the image reflected back; unable to look below the surface of her skin to explore the many qualities of self. When a woman develops projective objects in the creative process, she views the object with information derived from conscious awareness, as well as from places that are outside of conscious awareness. As she pulls information from the unconscious mind, she moves beneath the surface of the ocean water to explore the amazing, living world below. Her imagination is activated, metaphors come to life, and she begins to view herself and the world around her with the eyes of an artist.

In the preceding chapter, women also traveled into the world of the imagination where they explored self in the realm of images and symbols. Travelers took mental snapshots of their multi-sensory experience of standing near the ocean, and then created drawings to reflect that experience. Internal impressions and sensations of *being like the ocean* were moved to external expressions in the drawings. In this chapter, the metaphor of the ocean broadens to include an exploration of boats that sail upon the waters, and objects that exist around and below the surface of the water.

Women express curiosity and nervousness as they begin to explore the wide variety of art materials placed out on the tables. For many women, this is the first opportunity they have had to explore multi-media as an adult. The process may be reminiscent of childhood art projects when materials such as beads, cotton balls and tissue were used to make things like necklaces, bunnies and trees. Some travelers welcome childhood memories; some find the associations painful. Women are beginning to form a connection to the artist-identity, and eventually begin to relax in the creative atmosphere. The guide maintains the awareness of any participants who may be apprehensive, or having difficulty with directions or materials. She reminds travelers to practice the breathing and relaxation techniques introduced in the previous workshop.

Travelers begin the art process by creating boats that will carry them across the seas on the voyage of self-discovery. Although the image of a boat is not an actual representation of what the traveler sees when she looks in the mirror, she recognizes parts of herself symbolically depicted on the vessel she creates. Women relate to boats because of characteristics they have in common: both have physical bodies that allow for movement; their bodies contain internal machinery that drives the system; both require a mind operating at the helm in order to facilitate navigation through the waters; and they require communication capabilities to stay on course and connect to other boats on the waters. Women and boats are vessels; they are containers that move through life with purpose. Women and boats may be called upon to "hold" that which is needed to be held. Both are surrounded by life, and are able to sustain life by providing refuge and comfort to those who seek them out. Women and boats move forward into the unknown, even into the darkness where there is uncertainty, if there is a purpose for that voyage.

Each woman makes her own boat using standard white paper folded into an origami pattern. Origami is commonly associated with the Japanese culture. The art form reminds travelers that they are part of a broader world community; connected to other women of the world through exchanges of art and culture. The guide should develop comfort with this origami fold before presenting it to the group. Participants have their own copy of the origami pattern to work from; however, I have found that many women prefer to follow a step-by-step demonstration during the process. Women who feel comfortable working with the origami fold are encouraged to assist fellow travelers who need help. Women make the boats their own by adding words, images, objects and anything else they feel inspired to place on the paper vessels.

Once the boats are completed, participants create an anchor to travel with their ship. The anchor is a stabilizing device, used to restrict or prevent the motion of boats in stormy weather and turbulent waters. The anchor also helps to prevent an idling ship from drifting off course. Anchors, in varying degrees of shapes and sizes, are personalized so that they are as unique as the boats they accompany. Every woman has an anchor inside her own body, a place within that feels calm and peaceful. A woman's anchor has the ability to secure the body-vessel without holding it back from movement, if motion is desired. Women often describe feeling secure, centered or grounded in this anchored place within the body-vessel. Weary travelers often forget this place of refuge exists, or they may have difficulty locating their anchor. During this process, women identify the anchor within, and gain confidence that they can move to that place of security at any time.

Once the boats and anchors are created and ready for travel, participants move into the relaxation and guided imagery process. This exercise reinforces skills introduced in the previous chapter: breath awareness; tension and stress release; non-judgemental presence; and movement of thoughts and feelings through the mind and body. Once again, women shift into the world of the imagination where they explore their boat, the anchor they created and the anchor within. During the guided imagery process, the boats are imagined as life sized so they may be explored on a scale that complements the projective process. Many of the qualities women consider when they are looking at their vessel may be related to self as well: size; materials; colors; lines; age; vulnerability; personality; purpose; past injuries; seaworthiness; and location and purpose of anchor.

Following the relaxation and guided imagery exercise, travelers gather together for a group discussion. Participants practice speaking about self in the language of art and creativity, in the presence of other women. The guide encourages travelers to include positive statements about themselves as they process thoughts and feelings. Positive statements relating to self may seem like a foreign language to some women; however, participants become accustomed to this form of expression as they move through their journey of self-discovery. The practice of identifying and expressing positive thoughts and feelings about self creates an ideal bridge into the world of positive affirmations. Women take a few moments to develop an affirmation that speaks directly to the strengths of her boat. The affirmations should be brief, present-tense statements. For example, "I am strong and resilient as I move through the waters of life."

Although women travel alone in their boat-vessels out on the waters of life, they encounter other travelers on a regular basis. Boats may experience damage to their communication system and become disconnected from other vessels in the sea. Some women intentionally minimize or shut down contact with other travelers because they lack trust in the world around them. Women begin to repair or strengthen their connection to fellow travelers by working in small groups to create the waters of life. This art group is often the first one that women have ever participated in; therefore they are sailing into unknown territory with perceived risks to well-being. The guide may expect varying degrees of apprehension and/or resistance. Again, the guide maintains awareness of what appears to be happening in the room, and may step in to offer support if necessary. The guide reminds travelers of the calming techniques that they have learned along the way, and they are encouraged to practice these skills during the art process if needed.

As travelers join together in groups to create the waters of life that their boats will travel upon, they consider elements within and around the waters. These elements affect a traveler's perception of herself and the world around her. Some of those elements may be symbolically represented in the waters of life: opportunities and disappointments; joys and sorrows; obstacles and forms of assistance; and supportive people and people who hinder progress. Travelers anticipate times when the skies will be clear, the waters will be smooth, and sailing will seem effortless. They also consider times when clouds will loom overhead, waters will be choppy, and movement will seem difficult or impossible. The group explores symbols to represent potential climates and situations that take place out on the waters of life.

During the final process, each group member places her boat into the water, lowers the anchor and states her positive affirmation out loud. She is demonstrating a level of trust in her fellow travelers by sharing her vessel and her positive affirmation; both reflect personal information regarding how she perceives herself in the world. The guide encourages travelers to locate the anchors within their bodies. They take a moment to experience the sensation of security and peace originating from that place. The guide may choose to play music during this process; perhaps instrumental music with the sound of ocean waves in the background. The music reinforces breath awareness, and promotes the rhythmic flow of thoughts and feelings through the mind and body. Travelers become present in the moment, fully alive with all senses.

During this workshop, the gates of creativity open up so that ships may pass through into the world of the imagination. Travelers may desire further exploration of the ocean metaphor. The guide may extend the amount of time for the workshop to give women time to begin or complete an additional art project. Women may also work on this art project at home, in their own time. One significant benefit of working on the project at home is the reinforcement of art making as a form of relaxation and stress reduction. Engagement in the creative process promotes mindfulness; when the traveler is engaged in creativity, she is not worrying about things that have happened in the past, or what could possibly happen in the future. She is present with the art, in the here and now. The directive is simple: "Develop a three-dimensional scene of yourself standing near the ocean." I provide cardboard mandalas (circles) that can be used as a base for the project. I also provide plastic bags for participants to take some supplies with them. If art materials are limited, travelers are encouraged to use whatever supplies are available to them at home. The guide reminds travelers that objects found from nature (e.g. leaves, twigs, vines, etc.) are wonderful, cost-free art materials. The completed three-dimensional projects may be brought back for discussion before the experiential begins in Chapter 4.

Each traveler's boat has been shored up for travel upon the waters of life and has set sail on her maiden voyage. The women will find land and continue their journey of self-discovery on foot. The memories of today will remain with them; they will draw strength from their discoveries about self, and connection to other travelers. Travelers place the skills that they have learned into their backpacks, and set out to find the heroine within.

EXPERIENTIAL

Theme

The life journey continues and participants prepare to sail upon the open seas. The art and mindfulness experiential expands on a woman's ability to connect with the ocean as she seeks to learn more about herself and the world around her. Each participant creates a boat to represent the physical, emotional and spiritual qualities of self. The boats are equipped with anchors to assist with stability and grounding as they navigate the waters of life. Women work first individually, and then in small groups, as they continue the extraordinary journey of self-discovery.

Metaphors

Participants create boats from standard white paper and simple origami folds. A wide variety of art materials is used to personalize each boat to reflect "who I am" in the world.

Anchors are designed and developed to travel with the boats. The anchors provide a sense of security because they can be lowered into the water quickly. They provide stability for boats that have hit rough waters, and are in danger of capsizing or becoming lost at sea. Each participant will also locate an anchor somewhere inside her body. She can shift her attention to this grounding place to help manage sudden and/or unbearable waves of thoughts and feelings.

Relaxation and guided imagery promotes a calm, mindful presence in preparation for travel into the world of the imagination. Participants visualize the boat they created in the art process, and are guided in an in-depth exploration of the boat. During the relaxation and guided imagery process they are encouraged to continue the projective process, adding details to their boat as they picture themselves walking around it.

The waters of life represent the landscape of the journey itself. The waters may become choppy, tossing the boats around, perhaps throwing them off course. The waters may feel calm and peaceful at other times, promoting smooth sailing for the boats. The waters of life are filled with symbolic representations: comfort, aid and support (e.g. dolphins to help guide the boat, ports to stop for physical repair or refueling); obstacles, hardships and difficulties (e.g. sharp rocks, sharks in the water).

Objectives

- Women are invited to explore the art materials in the room. The facilitator explains that the art materials are used to enhance expression of thoughts and feelings.

- Participants engage in an art process to develop boats as projective representations of self. Women see themselves in a new way and are able to explore mind, body and spirit without judgement or criticism. This new perspective of self helps to challenge the consistent barrage of cultural messages that define worth based on expectations of outward appearance. Consideration of self as an artist and creator is consistently presented and practiced throughout the book.

- Reinforce the practice of relaxation and guided imagery (as introduced in this chapter) as a means to promote mindfulness in preparation for the journey into the world of the imagination. Thoughts, feelings and sensations are acknowledged and allowed to move away from the mind and body, like waves of the ocean. This process builds confidence that even the most difficult emotions can be safely managed.

- Establish a safe environment for women to explore the shame and grief that are commonly associated with perceived imperfections and shortcomings.

- Group members join together for the dialogue and reflection process.

- They practice speaking the language of self-affirmation in the presence of other women. Thoughts and feelings related to perceptions of self are explored; this creates a new frame of reference when conceptualizing "who I am" in the world.

- Develop a positive affirmation that speaks to the strength of the boat as it sails out on the waters of life.

- Working together in small groups, women create the Waters of Life. Participants hear contributions from other members relating to fear, trials, risks, courage, accomplishments and help from others when sailing out on the seas. This helps women to connect profoundly with other travelers.

Settings

ART PROCESS (BOAT AND ANCHOR)

Participants require adequate workspace to develop their boats as they work individually. A large table or flat surface is necessary for each group to create the Waters of Life. A chair should be available for each member; however, I also present the option of working while standing. A separate table for art materials is desirable. I always have a separate workstation for each warm glue gun.

RELAXATION AND GUIDED IMAGERY

Participants will need a space where they can sit in a chair or lie down while engaging in the relaxation and guided imagery process. I find it helpful to offer a low-light or adjusted light setting if possible. It is important to consider the possibility of interruptions ahead of time—you may want to place a "Do not disturb" sign on the door of the room you will be working in. Ask members to turn off their cell phones or other electronic devices to avoid distractions. Some type of music player is required if you decide to incorporate music into the process. Participants will need a table or solid surface to work on their drawings.

DIALOGUE AND REFLECTION

We can be as adaptive as we need to be; however, I have found that chairs set up in a circular setting reinforce the safe, comfortable setting required for group processing. Participants will need paper and a pen or pencil to write a positive affirmation.

- Music: The use of music is optional; however, I have found that instrumental sounds work very well with the boat and anchor experiential as well as the relaxation and guided imagery process. If you decide to incorporate music into any of the chapter experiential, consider a sound that blends instruments with the rhythm of the ocean waves.

- Art materials: The facilitator provides standard white paper (8½" × 11" (21.5 × 28cm)) and simple fold instructions (see Figure 3.1). You may prefer to use small, wood boats purchased from local craft stores and online suppliers. Other art materials include (but are not limited to): glue, glue guns, paints, markers, colored and decorative papers, glitter or glitter glue, beads, shells, ribbons and strings, tissue, cloth, clay and any found objects. Participants may also bring personal items from home that they would like to use in the art process.

Art Process

This art process incorporates the familiar concept of boat with the unfolding concept of self. The boats teach women how to look at "who I am" in the world, with less judgement and fear.

> Take some time (approximately five minutes) to explore the art materials in the room. Sometimes, art can say what the spoken language cannot say. Work with the art, and give it some of the control. Let the art help you express your thoughts and feelings.
>
> Using the paper and folding instructions that are set out on the table, create an origami boat (in approximately 15 minutes). Use the art materials to bring your boat to life as a representation of "who I am" in the world. Your boat should represent your physical body as well as emotional, intellectual and spiritual aspects of self. Try to consider, without judgement, qualities of self that you appreciate and value, as well as qualities that you ignore or reject. Create an anchor that will accompany your boat on its travels. Now imagine that your boat is an actual boat; life-sized and positioned so that you can walk all the way around it.

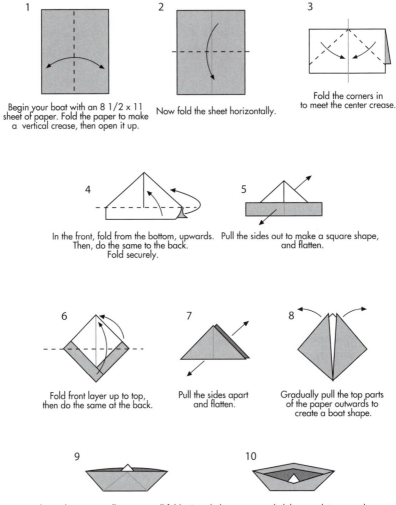

Figure 3.1 Folding instructions for origami boat

Relaxation and Guided Imagery Process

If you have time constraints, you may want to shorten the process by eliminating some of the considerations.

[Speak at a slow pace and allow for frequent pauses.]

Sitting on a chair, or on the floor, find a position that feels comfortable while keeping your neck and spine as straight as possible. Close your eyes. If you find that you are not comfortable closing your eyes, then focus on your boat and anchor in front of you. Take a deep, cleansing breath and be aware of how the air feels as it moves through your body, down into your abdomen. Feel the warmth and comfort of each breath. [pause] Stress and tension move out and away as you exhale, pushing the air all the way out. [pause] Continue breathing in and out, feeling your body relax. [pause] You are safe and accepted. Acknowledge any thoughts or feelings that come to mind, with peace, acceptance, and without judgement. [pause] Allow your thoughts and feelings to move through you, and away from you. [pause] Be aware of your presence in your chair, or on the floor, [pause] in this room, during this moment. [pause] You feel fully alive and relaxed. [pause] You are prepared to step into the world of the imagination; the world that is inside of you, waiting for you. [pause] Allow your mind's eye to picture the boat that you created today. [pause] Imagine that your boat is life-sized, [pause] and positioned so that you can walk all the way around it. Look at your boat, and pay close attention to anything that you see, even aspects of the boat that seem insignificant. [pause] If you would like to add anything to your boat, you may do so. [pause]

What is the structure of your boat? [pause] What are the textures that you see? [pause] What materials make up your boat? [pause] What colors do you see around the outside of your boat? [pause] Does the light, or lack of light, affect the colors of your boat? [pause] What are the lines that make up the form of your boat? [pause] Are they straight, curvy, circular...or formed in another way? [pause] What are the structural strengths and vulnerabilities of your boat? [pause] What is your sense of your boat standing alone...would it be strong? [pause] Would it be vulnerable? [pause] What would it be like for your boat to be surrounded by a few, or many, other boats? [pause] What descriptive words would you use to describe the personality of your boat? [pause] Does your boat seem to have a temperament, or a mood? [pause] What age does your boat appear to be? [pause] How is your boat similar to other boats? [pause] How is your boat unique? [pause] Does your boat seem to have a particular purpose? [pause] Who owns your boat? [pause] Who is at the helm of your boat? [pause] Has your boat experienced any trauma, or had to weather any significant storms, or been in any accidents? [pause] If so, can you see signs of the wounding beneath the touch-up? [pause] Overall, does your boat seem seaworthy? [pause] If you had the opportunity to shore your boat up to sail out on the waters of life, knowing that it is structurally sound, would you be able to tolerate the flaws and imperfections you see on the outside of your boat? [pause] As you get ready for your adventures out in the world, could you disregard the paint chipping away, or the faded color or rust that comes from years of travel and exposure to the elements? [pause] Could you acknowledge, and move beyond, the yearning for a newer, updated boat like the ones you see in the docks; knowing that newness cannot replace experience, familiarity and connection to other boats? [pause] Does any past wounding of the boat affect its ability to sail upon the waters? [pause] If so, what do you think your boat needs, and who can you ask for help? [pause] Some boats will require more attention before launching out onto the Waters of Life. Is your boat ready to sail, or does it need to be shored up in some way? [pause] If you feel your boat is seaworthy, and ready to go, are you prepared to take the helm to navigate the journey? [pause] How would your anchor help you to feel more secure as you sail along? [pause]

Now, with your mind's eye, examine the anchor you created. [pause] Walk around your anchor, and look at the lines, colors, materials and textures that form your anchor. [pause] Will your anchor be able to ground, or secure, your boat in the Waters of Life? [pause] Is there anything you would like to change about your anchor so it works in connection with your boat, and as effectively as possible? [pause] Now mentally search your own body until you find a place that feels grounded; a place that feels calm and secure; this can be anyplace in your body. [pause] If you have located this place within your body, imagine that it is a place where you will anchor yourself when you are experiencing waves of thoughts and feelings. [pause] You are able to go to this place quickly and effortlessly because it is always there, waiting for you. [pause] Feel the security of the anchor in your body. [pause] Your anchor grounds you, secures you, but does not drag you down, and you are able to move forward. If you have not identified this place within your body, that is okay, it will come to you. The next time you feel relaxed, imagine that you see the source of calmness within your body. This may be the place of your anchor.

Art Directive 1

Take a few moments to sketch your experience of the boat. Try to incorporate as many senses as possible: touch, smell, sight, sound, taste.

Dialogue and Reflection Process

Possible topics for discussion:

- What was it like to explore the art materials in the room? Were you drawn to any in particular?

- Did you feel any resistance to this part of the process? If so, how did you continue?

- How did you initially relate to your boat as a representation of "who I am" in the world? Did that change or shift as the process continued?

- Did you relate the body of your boat to your own body?

- What was it like to work in the presence of other women?

- Describe any feelings you experienced.

- Did you discover anything about yourself?

- Describe the positive qualities of self (mind, body and spirit) that are in your awareness now.

Positive Affirmation

Develop a positive affirmation about the ability of your boat-self to navigate through life. Write it down on a piece of paper. Example: "I am alive. I am strong and resilient. I endure storms on the water."

Develop a positive affirmation about your anchor and how it is associated with a safe place in your body: "I feel anchored in my chest and heart. I feel the life of my anchor. My anchor brings a sense of calm in the stormy seas." Write the affirmation down on a piece of paper and save it for later.

Art Directive 2

> Working in small groups, create the waters of life that your boats
> will travel upon. Consider all of the factors that may affect the pain
> and joy of the journey. [Read from the "Waters of Life" metaphors
> section to describe how symbols are used.]

Once "Waters of Life" is completed, individuals take turns placing
their boats in the water, lowering the anchors, while stating the
positive affirmation out loud. Each participant identifies a place in her
body where she can anchor herself when engulfed by negative body
image thoughts and feelings.

Additional Art Process

If time allows, I encourage women to make a three-dimensional
scene of themselves standing near the ocean (see Figure 3.2). I use a
cardboard mandala (circle) which may be purchased online or at many
local craft stores; I purchased mine from our local pizza parlor. If you
decide to buy them from a pizza parlor, make sure that they are the
flat mandalas.

Homework

> Place your boat and anchor (or an image of your boat and anchor)
> in a prominent place in your environment. Be sure to visit it daily
> for the next week and reflect on the positive aspects of this
> experience.

> Repeat your positive affirmations several times a day for the next
> week.

Art and Mindfulness

Artist's Statement

I am so happy I could do the origami fold. I wanted my ship to look
female. I wanted to remind myself that it is okay to be a grown-up girl.
I wanted lace and ribbon and shells. The shells represent my return
to the earth, back to the water one day. I am the salt of the earth.
Someday I will return. Today, I sail…with gladness.

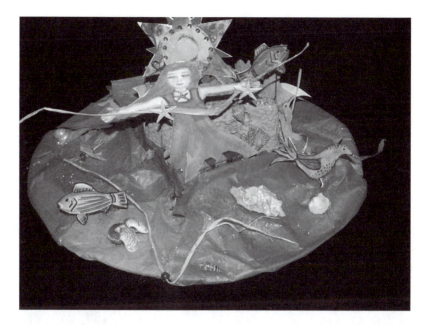

Figure 3.2 Mermaid

Figure 3.3 A girl's boat

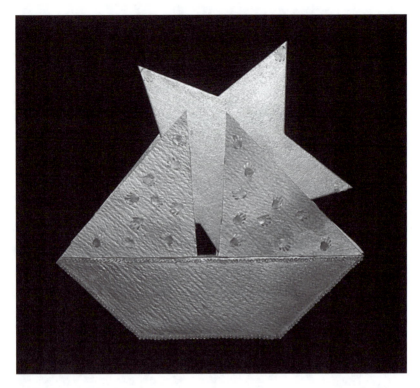

Figure 3.4 Many hands boat

4

The Heroine's Journey

Finding Hope and Strength from Within

INTRODUCTION

While traveling along the road of life, women encounter ordinary people who do extraordinary things to assist others. At times, these helpers risk their own well-being to ensure the safety and survival of fellow travelers. Our culture acknowledges heroism in stories and representations of women from history, as well as in larger-than-life characters depicted in comics, movies, video games, music and other pop culture forms of entertainment. In real life, women who serve in the military or work as first responders are considered heroic because of the risks they assume to protect and rescue others. Women who work in helping professions are recognized as heroic when lives are improved or saved in environments which present particular challenges or dangers.

Women are much less familiar with the concept of the hero within, the remarkable self that faces and overcomes obstacles on a daily basis. In heroine development, we face the deeper issues that underlie the physical, emotional and spiritual struggles encountered on the road of life. What trials would the heroine-self be willing to undergo in order to bring profound and sustainable change to her life? What obstacles would the heroine-self be willing to face, knowing the risks involved? In this version of the heroine's journey, women create *wands* to carry with them as they move forward to answer these questions.

The wands are companions that represent the presence of hope and strength during times of suffering. In the well-known "hero's journey" described by Joseph Campbell (2008), the hero first experiences a call to adventure. Throughout history, ordinary and extraordinary women have responded to such a call in order to improve or save the lives of other human beings—women such as Harriet Tubman, Anne Frank,

Rosa Parks, Eleanor Roosevelt, Princess Diana and Mother Teresa are just a few well-known women who are considered heroic because of the way they lived their lives. Although their causes and methods may have differed significantly, each one was able to cast light into the shadows of human suffering and despair.

A heroine's words, acts and visions for a better world inevitably surpass how she *looked* as she walked through the world. This is often true regardless of how much, or little, physical beauty she was determined to have possessed for herself. Heroines teach us about courage, hope, compassion, resiliency and the power of the human spirit to triumph over adversity.

The larger-than-life heroines we see in popular internet and video games are meant to stimulate a visual response that holds the viewer's interest. Youthful heroines such as Celes from "Final Fantasy VI," and Lara Croft from "Tomb Raider," reflect a stylized form of female beauty. The heroines' hair, lips, hips and breasts are highlighted so they may be viewed, and experienced, as sexual objects under the control of the male gamer. Female gamers may have a greater sense of working in partnership with these female characters throughout the course of games. Although women express some interest in the physical appearance of the heroines, they seem to have greater interest in other qualities that are unrelated to their physical beauty.

If we look beyond the unrealistic bodies of the characters, we may discover traits that are relevant to heroism: intelligence; physical strength and athletic prowess, martial arts and weapons skills; ability to work with others on a team; communication skills; a sense of feeling empowered as equal with men; and confidence that comes from the feeling of having a sense of control. The strengths may be symbolically depicted by means of accessories such as capes, warrior boots, belts, weaponry, staffs or wands.

Hollywood creates heroines to complement pop culture trends. These heroines often possess incredible physical and/or supernatural powers. Buffy the Vampire Slayer, Wonder Woman and Charlie's Angels are able to battle criminals and evildoers, while maintaining a sense of style, beauty and sex appeal. Actresses in the roles of heroines who tackle real-life issues often meet or transcend Western cultural standards of beauty. Jennifer Lopez empowers herself as she combats her abusive husband in the movie "Enough"; Julia Roberts champions a major environmental cause in her role as "Erin Brockovich"; and

Sandra Bullock brings attention to the issue of caring for homeless children in the movie "Blindside." In some cases, the actresses are portraying actual women who also meet or surpass cultural standards of beauty. The questions remain: "Are heroic, real-life women who are not considered to be attractive by Western cultural standards being adequately represented in television and movies? Are Western women being conditioned to believe that a woman must be beautiful in order to be heroic? How does the average woman define herself as she walks through the world? Does she ever see her daily actions as having heroic qualities?"

A woman's definition of self is derived, in part, from the works that she does for others out in the world. She may bear responsibility for the care of family members or loved ones. Care within the home environment may include: food preparation, shopping, housework, transportation, appointment tracking, nursing, care of the pets, gardening, help with homework, education of children, bathing and grooming of children, managing finances, attending medical appointments, coaching, and coordination of extra-curricular activities. A woman may be called upon to perform these duties after a long day of work or school, or a combination of both.

Women often avail themselves to friends and family members outside of the home as well. Just when a woman thinks that her physical and emotional reserves are completely depleted, she receives a call from a friend asking for assistance or support. Women are helping women get through medical treatments and divorces. They cook and deliver meals for friends who have lost family members, and stay on the phone for lengthy periods of time to reassure friends having problems with children. Women baby boomers are helping to care for parents who wish to stay at home as they advance in age. Women are called upon, perhaps now more than ever, to help others.

Female travelers commonly interpret their role as *caregiver* to mean that attention must be given to the endless need encountered on their life courses. Women are often selfless in their outreach to others, and services are frequently delivered without anticipation of reciprocation or recognition.

Many women embrace their natural desire to assist others because of the connection that takes place in the process. However, increasing numbers of Western women are becoming weary and sad. A major contributing factor to the physical and mental health of women is the increased level of stress resulting from trying to do too much, for too long. The demands made on a woman frequently extend beyond her physical and/or mental ability to deliver. She walks through the world as an ordinary woman facing extraordinary circumstances. She is a heroine in her own right. Yet she is more likely to criticize herself for not being able to do enough, rather than recognize her own amazing qualities. Weighed down by heavy emotions, she neglects to reach out to others who may help *her*. She may also disregard, or be unaware of, the internal resources that lie within her. When a woman feels a sense of despair or loss of control in her external environment, she may compensate by attempting to control what she eats, what she weighs and how she appears to others as she walks through the world.

During the "Heroine's Journey" process, the simple act of acknowledging hardships and suffering faced while traveling the road of life brings hope for the possibility of movement and transformation. Lack of validation causes women to step aside, or retreat, in search of safety and some form of comfort. The Heroine's Journey helps each woman step back onto the road to see her life journey with new eyes: the eyes of a heroine.

One of the women who walked along the road with our group was able to teach fellow travelers about courage as she faced the end of her life. She developed, and integrated, her own story of a heroine on a life adventure. As her physical health declined, she was able to grieve the impending loss of life, while living her life to the fullest in each moment that remained. She found heroic qualities within herself that helped her face and resolve problems with her son. She taught the people around her that internal strength is obtainable, even when the life journey is coming to an end. She playfully incorporated some of the classic qualities of stereotypical heroines into her artwork: a cape, a superhero belt buckle and a heroine's wand that she used in guided imagery to help manage her diseased cells. When she developed her heroine wand, she expressed amazement at her own ingenuity and creativity. She found metaphors in images and materials to represent the strengths that she carried within. She kept the heroine wand she made close to her at nights so she could visualize her heroine-self traveling through her body, communicating to her cells and organs. She became a heroine in our group because of her concern for other group members and her determination to help them understand that they should appreciate their bodies because they "only get one for life." She attended the group until the near end of her life.

The Heroine's Journey does not promote a disregard for the reality of what women are actually facing in life; rather the journey strengthens a woman's belief that she can fully experience all of her emotions while she continues to live and love. The supportive group environment reinforces her sense of worthiness to receive help from others. The guide, group and the artwork itself mirror back qualities of self that exist beneath the surface of the skin. The heroine wand that is developed is not magical in the usual sense of the word. The magic comes from the transformation that takes place when travelers begin to appreciate their own self-worth. As transformation occurs, lives begin to change. This is an amazing process to witness.

EXPERIENTIAL

Theme
The heroine's journey takes participants on a journey of self-discovery in search of the heroine within. Travelers have already been introduced to the process of relaxation and guided imagery in preparation for travels into the world of the imagination, where symbols, metaphors and stories come to life. Heroines will create a heroine wand to carry with them on their life journeys.

Metaphors
The concept of *hero* or *heroine* is one that women often recognize in larger-than-life figures, in people who are called upon to assist other people in extraordinary ways, or in the lives of other women who work in the helping professions. In this art process, women are introduced to the heroine within, the remarkable self that faces and overcomes obstacles on a day-to-day basis.

Women embrace the heroine's wand, which could be considered to be a symbol representative of male strength, as they identify their own qualities associated with strength. They also consider qualities in others that they may want to develop for themselves. The wands represent the qualities that women would like to carry with them on their journey of self-discovery.

Wands carried by heroes and wizards are sometimes associated with the concept of magic that is derived outside of the self. The heroine wands are associated with magic that comes from internal transformation, and external movement and growth. The act of caring for oneself is magical.

Objectives

- Reinforce relaxation and guided imagery with the theme of identifying heroic qualities within the self. The relaxation and guided imagery reinforces management of difficult emotions that may arise in the art process.

- Participants practice a multi-sensory mindful presence before beginning the art process.

- Participants engage in dialogue with other women to practice hearing their own voice speak about qualities of self in an open and genuine way. This provides an introduction to the culture of positive self-affirmation that continues in the following chapters. Women also consider qualities they admire in other women—they learn that they can admire traits of women without necessarily "liking" those women.

- Participants engage in the art process, to develop wands based on heroic qualities that they have identified within themselves, or would like to develop within themselves.

Settings

Selection of a Heroine Wand

Place wooden dowels around the room (different sizes if possible) and instruct participants to select a wand when they come into the room.

Relaxation and Guided Imagery

Provide a quiet space for participants to sit or lie down on the floor while engaging in the relaxation and guided imagery process. Offer adjusted light if possible. Consider placing a "Do not disturb" sign on the door to avoid interruptions.

I have a small collection of female action figure heroines that I place around the room as inspiration. You may also place images of real-life female heroines on the walls of tables. Select women from different walks of life.

- Art materials: Facilitator provides wooden dowels (approximately 2" wide and 30" long). (Participants have requested longer dowels so that they have full-size wands.) I try to provide a variety of lengths of dowels. I provide eye hooks for the end of the dowels so that strings may be attached if desired. Other art materials include (but are not limited to):

  - items from nature such as feathers; leaves; shells; natural strings; and any other found or purchased objects associated with nature

  - glue; glue guns; glitter glue

  - paints; markers

  - ribbons; sturdy and delicate strings

  - cloth.

I have discovered that women get very creative with this project. One participant placed an old camera and vintage eyeglasses on her wand.

Relaxation and Guided Imagery Process

> *[Speak at a slow pace and allow for frequent pauses.]*
>
> Find a position that feels comfortable for you, and close your eyes. If you are not comfortable closing your eyes, then please focus on the heroine wand that figures on the table. [pause] Notice your breath as it moves in and out of your body. [pause] You feel light and comfortable. [pause] You are ready to transition into the world of the imagination, the home of symbols, myths and stories. [pause] Feel yourself present in the moment, open to thoughts, ideas, feelings and memories that may come forward. Anything that comes into the conscious mind, you allow to move through—like leaves blowing over the grass, or clouds moving through the sky. You feel safe and relaxed as you inhale [pause] and exhale. [pause]
>
> Take a few moments to think about qualities of heroism that you recognize in characters on television shows, movies and comic books. [long pause] Allow the images of those women to enter into your mind. [pause] What do you notice about the woman, or women, that you see? [pause] Do they have capes, special belts, boots or headgear? [pause] What are the colors that you see?

[pause] Focus on one heroine. [longer pause] What position is she in… Is she standing with her hands on her hips, as if ready to take on the world? [pause] Is she preparing to fly? [pause] Or is she in some completely different position or pose? [pause] What is her facial expression? [pause] What does that facial expression tell you about her attitude or determination? [pause] What qualities of this heroine would you like to take with you to carry on your voyage of self-discovery? [long pause]

Now imagine real women that you admire, and see as potential heroines out in the world. [pause] These can be women that you know or don't know. [pause] They may be family members, community members or members of the broader world community. [pause] Take a moment to picture these women. [long pause] Focus on one woman who has qualities that you admire and consider heroic. [longer pause] Take a moment to notice her physical appearance. [pause] Now look deeper into her eyes and her facial expression. [pause] What does her face say about her? [pause] Do you see any qualities such as wisdom determination or compassion? [pause] Look at her body language—what does the way that she holds herself, carries herself or positions herself say about who she is in the world? [longer pause]

Take a few moments to picture yourself, first as a superhero character. [pause] Imagine the outfit you would wear. [pause] Let your imagination have fun with the image of what you would look like as a superhero. [pause]

Now imagine yourself as a real woman in the world. [pause] Look at your physical appearance for a moment. [pause] Now imagine yourself looking into your own eyes. [pause] Imagine yourself in a situation where you might be called upon for help or assistance. [pause] What is your facial expression? [pause] What emotions show in your eyes and face? [pause] Where is the strength in your body [pause]…your mind [pause]…your spirit? [pause]

Imagine all of the qualities that you have visualized in this process. Imagine the qualities that belong to the heroine characters, the real-life women, and yourself. [long pause] You will bring those qualities back to the room, and represent them on your heroine wand.

When you are ready, return to the room and open your eyes.

We will take a couple of minutes to remain seated (or lying down). [pause] Feel yourself present in the room. [pause] You are aware of thoughts and feelings that come into your mind and body; you acknowledge them and allow them to move through. [long pause] Feel your experience of being fully alive, in this room, on this day. [pause] Explore your experience in this room with all of your senses. [pause]

When you are ready, you may move into the group discussion circle.

Dialogue and Reflection Process 1

Move into a group setting for the dialogue and reflection process. Women are encouraged to use their voices by sharing their thoughts and feelings related to the relaxation and guided imagery process.

Possible questions for discussion:

- What was it like to relax and breathe?

- Were you able to allow thoughts and feelings to come and go?

- Which heroines did you imagine?

- Did you consider any women that you don't particularly like, or have trouble getting along with?

- What were some of the qualities of heroism that you discovered?

- How did you see yourself?

- Which qualities of heroism did you bring back to represent on your wand?

Art Process

Use a variety of materials to develop a heroine's wand that you will carry with you on your journey of *self-discovery*. Consider all of the qualities of heroism that you identified during the relaxation and guided imagery process. It is okay if you do not have these qualities. Consider traits that you would like to incorporate into your own way of being in the world. This wand belongs to you—it should be as unique as you are. Continue to let your thoughts and feelings come and go as you work on this process. Allow yourself to be fully present in the moment; alive with all of your senses.

Dialogue and Reflection Process 2

Possible questions for discussion:

- Describe the process of creating a wand.

- Were there any women, in particular, that you thought of while creating your wand?

- Which heroic qualities did you include on your wand? Why?

- Was there anything you considered and then decided not to include?

- How will your wand assist you on your journey?

Homework

Place your wand next to your bed at night—make sure it is visible. Practice the relaxation technique you have learned. Begin to imagine your own heroine's journey. Picture yourself carrying your wand into a land where your heroic qualities are used and appreciated. Write the story in your journal.

The Heroine Wand

Artist's Statement

I loved doing the Heroine Wand project because it was in a group full of beautiful and inspiring women. For me, the process seemed so much more strengthening that way. I remember deconstructing Christmas baubles and wiring them together into a linear form.

The designer smiles (in type) that were encapsulated at the base of the wand kinda makes me cringe, kinda not. One of the saddest things I can think of is a forced smile. With all the alterations to self we encounter, sometimes the most reinforcing thing we can experience is a genuine smile and a great belly laugh.

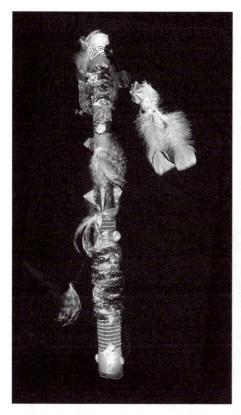

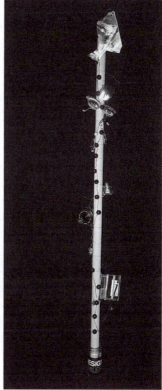

Figure 4.1 Shells and feathers

Figure 4.2 Heroine wand

5

Notion of Emotions

Rating Intensity and Environmental Influence

INTRODUCTION

The journey of self-discovery continues and participants pause for a rest, in order to gather strength and resources for the ongoing voyage. The guide (facilitator) informs the travelers that they may face choppy waters and rough roads ahead as they face feelings and emotions that directly impact body image. The travelers gather supplies that will help them navigate their vessels through stormy weather, and obstacles on the roadways. The women have practiced a mindful awareness of being present in the moment, fully alive with all senses. They have imagined the sound of ocean waves while allowing thoughts and feelings to move through the mind and body. They have identified the anchor within the body; the place that provides a sense of stability and groundedness. They carry their wands as reminders of the heroine within. All of these tools will help the travelers manage difficult emotions associated with exploration of self, particularly the body-self.

Although there are differences in definition and meaning between *feelings* and *emotions*, they are used interchangeably in this process. Women explore feelings that are immediate and transient in nature, as well as emotions that are deeply rooted and lasting. There are many factors that affect the way feelings and emotions are experienced: the ability to recognize and name different feelings and emotions, interpretation of feelings and emotions, and fear or acceptance of having either. Environmental factors along the waters and roads of life contribute to the intensity of the emotional experience. In the "Notion of Emotions" process, travelers gain greater awareness of external stimuli that initiate feelings and contribute to prolonged emotional states. When a traveler feels that she has acquired skills that help her identify and manage emotions, she moves forward with confidence in her ability to navigate through any difficulties encountered along the way.

The experience of exploring body image is the experience of exploring self, profoundly and completely. This process initiates strong emotional responses at times. Memories associated with current and past relationships are brought forward in images and stories. Accounts of life events weave into the tapestry that becomes the present experience. Emotions associated with memories of people, places and things are acknowledged in the mind and body, and then released. A traveler is not always able to avoid factors that initiate emotional distress; however, she considers the likelihood of encountering certain environmental stimuli on known courses. She will be given opportunities to select specific paths, and her ability to make choices and decisions promotes a sense of active participation in her life journey. She is able to take control of her vessel to steer towards the direction of personal growth.

In the "Notion of Emotions" process, participants gather to discuss the course of the journey of self-discovery. The guide pulls out a map and explains that there will be stops along the roadway so that travelers may acquire items needed for the journey. Participants will develop their own purses and shoes that will travel with them. They will interact with a nostalgic doll who will be given a voice to speak her truth. The voice belongs to the women on the journey; they will practice sharing thoughts and feelings in the presence of other women. Further down the road, travelers will encounter art processes that promote exploration of the actual body-self. The guide reassures the women that they will continue to develop coping skills along the way. She reminds them that they are not alone on the journey.

During this art process, travelers increase knowledge of their emotional states by creating a *visual rating scale*. Participants draw a line on a long piece of paper and identify a continuum of emotional intensity: *slight, medium* and *maximum*. Each woman selects an image (from magazines) that represents an emotion she has experienced recently. The image is glued onto the paper (scale), at a point that represents the intensity of the emotion. Images that represent greater and lesser intensity levels of that same emotion are placed on the scale as well. Throughout the process, travelers are encouraged to locate the experience of the emotions in their bodies as they continue to practice allowing them to move through. Images are also used to represent feelings that were present *before* and *after* the identified emotion. Participants select images to characterize environmental influences that impact intensity of the emotions.

I had the opportunity to walk with a young woman named Emily on the journey of self-discovery. By the time we had arrived at the "Notion of Emotions" process, Emily felt strengthened by the skills she had learned along the way. She felt especially empowered by the heroine's wand that she created because it was a tangible representation of her own strength. Emily always had difficulty with strong feelings and emotions. She said she had a tendency to "eat everything in sight" when she couldn't tolerate her feelings. This brought temporary comfort, and a lasting sense of self-contempt. After a binge, Emily would spend hours focusing on her body fat while feelings of being "selfish" and "bad" engulfed her mind. In the workshop she identified "anger" as an emotion she felt often. She considered avoiding use of this feeling in this process because she wanted to hold on to the full intensity of the anger. She said her anger felt protective. If this process had been the first one in the book, I believe Emily would have avoided exploring her anger. However, she had traveled the waterways and roads with her fellow travelers; she believed that they would offer validation and support in the process. She had been practicing her homework, and felt it was possible to "try" to manage difficult emotions. This step launched Emily onto the roadways which led to feelings of confidence and vulnerability.

Emily's picture was not available for reproduction; however, the images she used are easily described and imagined. She chose an image of a dark and active thunderstorm to represent her anger. That image was placed on the *maximum* intensity section of her scale. She chose an image of a rainy day to place in the *medium* intensity section, and an image of a storm off in the distance to represent the *slight* intensity experience of anger. Emily identified "shame" as the emotion she experienced before her anger, and "self-hatred" as the one that followed. She placed pictures of her family members throughout her scale: people she felt cared about her and helped her, and others who she felt were harmful to her. She realized that the presence of her uncle (who had molested her as a child) initiated her sense of shame, which led to anger, and ultimately self-hatred. She was able to identify all of these feelings within her body, and move them through with techniques she had practiced.

Like the other travelers on that day, Emily developed a sense of mastery: she was able to identify her feelings and name them; she moved her internal experience to the external world as she explored feelings and emotions in images. She utilized breathing and multi-sensory mental images of ocean waves to move her feelings through her mind and body. She gained a sense of direction as she understood the environmental impact on emotions. Like the other travelers on that day, Emily took her notion of emotions and set back out on the road to self-discovery.

Women who are dealing with body image concerns are often disconnected from their emotional experiences, in the same way as they have become detached from the experience of their bodies. The mind's ability to identify the location of a feeling in the body is essential in its ability to restore order and calm to the system. If a traveler is carrying frustration in her stomach and chest, and her mind does not connect to the feeling, then she may perceive the upset in her stomach as a hunger cue. She may interpret the movement in her chest as the beginning of a heart attack. The woman may become even more frustrated when food and/or pain reliever bring only short-lasting relief to the system. Until she is able to identify emotions, and understand factors that help to sustain them, she may have difficulty moving forward on her life journey.

Each traveler on the journey of self-discovery picks up her visual rating scale that serves as an emotional compass, places it into her backpack with other supplies she has attained, and moves forward to fulfill her destiny.

EXPERIENTIAL

Theme

The traveler on the voyage of self-discovery seeks additional skills that she can carry in her backpack and pull out to use when needed. She knows that difficult emotions have the potential to create stormy weather, or block the roadways up ahead. She is introduced to a visual rating scale that will help her identify and manage emotions that she encounters along the way.

Metaphors

The *visual rating scale* is made up of images taken from books and magazines. The traveler selects pictures as representations of emotions, people and situations.

The rating scale itself serves as a type of compass, helping travelers find their way through emotional states.

Objectives

- Provide a brief resting period for travelers so they may regroup and plan for the roads ahead.

- Women work individually in the art process and then gather for dialogue in a group setting. They receive validation and support from the guide and fellow travelers.

- The *visual rating scale* enhances a traveler's ability to identify her own emotional states and increases her awareness of the variations in the intensity of all emotions. She learns that thoughts and feelings are fluid: they move through the mind and body when allowed to do so.

- Participants acknowledge feelings that come before and after identified emotions. These feelings are also rated in intensity.

- Travelers explore environmental factors that impact the intensity of emotions, and gain confidence in their ability to handle difficult emotions and situations that may lie ahead.

Settings

ART PROCESS

Participants will need adequate workspace to develop their collage images. Women may sit together at round tables or a long table, so they can share magazines placed in the center of the table. Some kind of music player is required if you decide to incorporate music in the process.

DIALOGUE AND REFLECTION

Clients will require seating for the dialogue and reflection process. If possible, place chairs in a circle so members are able to look at each other during the discussion.

- Music:

  ○ Benefits of using music: Initiates emotional response. May be calming, soothing, in the process, depending on the music.

  ○ Reason to exclude music: Some songs or pieces may initiate specific emotions as memories of people, places and things may be associated with the music. This is a process that promotes awareness of the moment that travelers are in.

- Art materials: Provide long pieces of white paper. Have a wide variety of magazines available. You will need glue and/or glue sticks and scissors for this process.

Initial Discussion

Travelers gather together to discuss an important aspect of the human experience: emotions. The guide reminds participants of the skills they have learned so far. They are able to acknowledge feelings, and then allow them to move through the mind and the body. They have practiced becoming grounded in a multi-sensory experience of being like the ocean. Women apply positive affirmations: "I feel strong; I am safe; I am supported and cared for; I am managing difficult emotions."

Possible topic and questions for discussion:

- Try to think of a time on this journey when you felt a strong emotion.

- What was that emotion? Was this the initial emotion, or was there another one that came first? Was there an emotion that came after?

- Go back to the first emotion that you thought of. As you were experiencing that emotion, did it seem to change in intensity at all? (This could mean less intense, or more intense.)

- Did you notice how the emotion changed?

- Do you recall feeling the emotion in your body?

- If so, did the intensity of the emotion increase or decrease in your body?

- Was there anything that helped you manage the emotions?

Art Process

Draw a line on a piece of paper—this line will develop into a visual rating scale to help you identify the range of emotional intensity. Write the word "slight" at one end, the word "medium" in the middle and the word "maximum" at the other end of the paper. Next, try to think of an emotion that you have had recently.

Pay attention to the experience of this emotion in your body. Remember to breathe, and relax, as you allow the feeling to move through your body.

Select an image from the magazines that represents the emotion. Place it on the scale at a point that indicates the intensity of the emotion.

Next, select images that represent the *slight, medium* and *maximum* intensity of the emotion. Place the images wherever you think they belong on the scale.

Look at the image of the emotion you placed on the paper and try to imagine what feelings came before and after this emotion. For example, if you selected "doubt" as the initial emotion, then "confusion" may be the feeling that came before, and "anger" may be the emotion that followed. (These are just examples.)

Select images that represent environmental factors, such as people, places, things or situations that may impact intensity of the emotions. Place those images on the scale in relation to the emotions they affect.

Dialogue and Reflection Process

Possible questions for discussion:

- What was the initial emotion that you thought of?

- Did you experience this emotion in your body?

- Did it change in intensity at all?

- Did you have a sense of other feelings/emotions before or after this one?

- Did you experience those emotions in your body?

- Were you able to practice calming techniques that you learned in previous experientials?

- What were some of the environmental factors that impacted the intensity of your emotions?

- What would you like to share about your *visual rating scale?*

Homework

Place your artwork in a visible location. As you walk by your visual rating scale, look at the emotions that you depicted, and feel the fluidity of those emotions. They are moving, shifting in intensity. Take a moment to become aware of your breath moving in and out of your body as you inhale and exhale. Imagine your body as being like the ocean: feelings and emotions come in, and move away, like the waves. You may wish to continue to add images to your piece.

Notion of Emotions

Artist's Statement

I put lines going up and down in my picture because my emotions never feel like they move in a straight line. As I started to think about things that cause a little stress, I began to feel the stress in my body. As I moved up the scale to feel things that cause moderate feelings, I began to feel stronger feelings in my body. I took time to breathe and I let the feelings move away from me. I put in social aspects of my life that cause my feelings to become stronger (happy and sad). I'm glad I knew I could breathe, and imagine waves of the ocean to calm my feelings down.

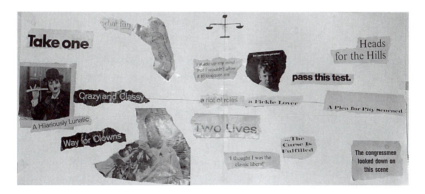

Figure 5.1 Menopause

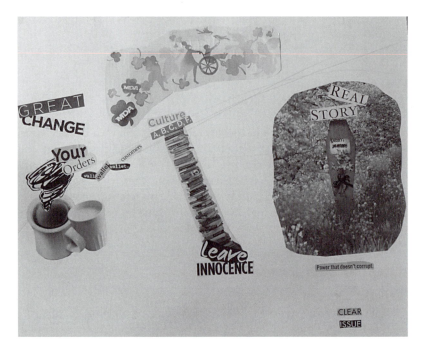

Figure 5.2 Hardworking college girl

Figure 5.3 My ups and downs

6

A Woman's Purse

Reflection of Self

INTRODUCTION

It takes a brave or foolish soul to try to separate a woman from her purse (or handbag). We have seen the cartoons and video clips of the woman struggling to fight off the would-be robber as he attempts to relieve her of her bag. A woman's natural, protective instincts seem to apply to her handbag the same way that they apply to protection of her family and those that she loves.

It could be argued that there are few, if any, personal belongings that a woman can form a relationship with. However, any woman who has carried a contraption that holds her valued possessions knows that it is truly possible to form an intimate, interactive bond with a purse. Interactive? Yes, interactive. A woman regularly relates to her purse utilizing a multi-sensory approach that includes an instinctual expectation that the purse will relate back. And purses do seem to relate back!

If walls could talk they would tell stories of women who walk into rooms seeking a safe resting place for their handbag. They would notice that most of the time the purses cooperate with the woman's choice of space; however, some bags have been known to resist by refusing to bend or fold into the chosen spot. Even so, with gentle encouragement and skilled hands a woman can often convince her purse to comply.

The walls might describe the woman's parting—hesitant glances during the difficult separation period, particularly as she deposits her purse in a safe place, before exiting the room. There is much that happens between drop-off and pick-up of the purse that the walls cannot see. For instance, the walls cannot see the images of the purse that drift in and out of the mind's eye of the woman as she sits in her meeting or appointment. Dreamy impressions of her purse are commonly accompanied by anticipation that she will soon be reunited with her companion and they will travel on together.

The walls see the woman return for her purse with sharp, focused eyes that quickly and efficiently seek out the location of this familiar and comforting object. She approaches with a softness or hardness of touch depending on her mood or her schedule, and more often than not the purse yields submissively.

Familiar smells may arise from her purse as she opens it, and she subconsciously experiences a sense of gratitude that she has a loyal vessel to guard her gum, lotion and other scented items.

The woman also relates to sounds that her purse makes. She identifies with the steady and reassuring noise of the zipper as it moves across the tops or sides of the purse, the gentle clinking of the metal objects hanging from various parts of the purse, and the swish of the material as the purse is lifted and shifted into alignment with the movement of the woman. This is an intimate, interactive dance that begins as a rite of passage into young adulthood and often lasts for a lifetime.

The ability of the purse to evoke strong emotional responses from women became apparent to me during the first purse art workshop I facilitated several years ago. I was taken by surprise as I witnessed women recalling memories of their mothers, grandmothers and other women in their lives, as they handled the vintage purses that had been donated for the project. Initially, the purses had been placed around the room and the women were asked to select a purse that they seemed to have some connection with. This directive was deliberately kept very broad and open to interpretation by each member.

The room became silent as the women began to roam around, first looking casually at all of the bags from a distance, and then moving in closer to examine a bag they felt drawn to. The sounds of the purses being picked up, turned around, opened and repositioned seemed to form a familiar melody that accompanied soft steps and careful movements. It felt as if we were in a world within a world.

Once each woman identified her purse, she moved to a chair within a circle of chairs. The group soon became wrapped in nostalgia as each member took her turn describing reasons for selecting her purse. The women began to tell stories of other women that we would likely never meet—many who were no longer living. We heard stories about loss and gain, tragedy and triumph, fear and courage. We heard about the complexities of relationships, financial hardships, travels, jobs, roles in the family and society, as well as dreams and letting go of dreams. We listened to women talking about temperaments, intelligence, body features and illnesses, both mental and physical.

Group members became emotional when describing their memories of what each of these women had carried in her purse. They recalled the smells of minty gum mixed with nicotine, hankies ironed with starch and scented with lilac, perfumes like "Evening in Paris," "Moonwind" and "Chanel No. 5," and cherry lifesavers. They remembered compacts and lipsticks, pictures and letters, checkbooks and bills, stamps and keys. They used words and phrases like: unique, educated, homemaker, strong, fragile, attitude, abused, assertive, gentle, punishing, ahead of her time. The purses initiated a recollection of the spirit or essence of women who had made a lasting impression on each group member.

I asked each participant to remove an object from her own purse that she would be willing to share with the group. The members would later speak to thoughts that shifted from perception of other women to perception of self: how would others in the room perceive them, and how would they be described by others in the future, based on what they carried in their purses today? They chose carefully. The items were as diverse as the women who formed our group on that day. We were introduced to a gold pen that was pulled from the purse of a woman who was constantly trying to find a way to fit art into her life; a pocket knife from the purse of a woman who wanted to feel some sense of safety always; a small charm that was worn and dull from rubbing, passed down from a grandmother, pulled from the purse of a woman who called upon maternal comfort in times of stress. Other women pulled out objects related to relationships, interests and responsibilities.

One by one, as each group member spoke about the item she had selected, curiosity seemed to wash away any apprehension of judgement from others. Instead, questions about the objects themselves: Why was she carrying this item in her purse? Where did it come from and how long had she had it? What was her attachment to the object, or what would it be like to lose the object? They tried to remember who else knew about the object. If someone found the object, what might they glean about the person who carried it?

Discussion of the objects that had been raised from silent resting places within the purses seemed to offer each woman a new and unexpected perspective of herself and her life. Free from the limitations of personal evaluation based on what a mirror reflects back, the women explored: values, goals, creativity and intelligence, determination, ability to face obstacles, as well as intuition, assertiveness, humor and communication. They considered their roles as mothers, daughters, wives and partners.

The women moved easily and quietly into the art process. Exploration of the purses and objects within the purses seemed to create a natural bridge from the world of self-discovery to the world of self-expression. I watched for signs of confusion as I gave the directive: "Create a purse that reflects who you are." However, the women moved immediately to the art material table and began to transform the bags which they had chosen. The women also began creating objects to go inside of their purses, and were encouraged to consider this as an ongoing process that could continue beyond this workshop experience.

During the day's final process period, some of the women expressed appreciation for their purses. They felt that the purses had promoted a greater understanding and appreciation of self, reflecting and containing valuable information about each woman. Such information could be passed down from generation to generation if desired. The bags suddenly appeared to be *functional art*, bringing an exciting new meaning to the concept of accessorizing. The purses had also broadened the women's concepts of themselves as artists. This new identity was apparent in the way they held their purses as they walked out of the building, back into the world.

I am frequently asked if artistic talent is required for this workshop, and I explain that any woman can participate. A curiosity to understand the creative process, and a willingness to participate, are all that is really required. When working with less experienced groups, I do brief demonstrations showing use of some of the materials. This seems to help promote a sense of safety and comfort. I am also available to answer questions or to help with art material problem solving if necessary. This process and its various outcomes will be unique in many ways for each woman. That is how we like it. That's what makes the purse so personal.

EXPERIENTIAL

Theme

The journey of self-discovery continues as travelers create a functional accessory to carry along the way. This chapter begins with a relaxation and guided imagery exercise to help bridge memories of women and their purses from the past, to greater awareness of *self* in the present. The mind's eye images of the purses evoke strong memories of mothers, grandmothers and other significant women who in some way influenced the life of each participant. Recollection of personal items that were carried in the purses promotes a greater sense of *who* the woman was as she traveled on her life journey

Metaphors

Purses are accessories that are commonly carried by women as they walk through life. Handbags are often carefully selected by women to signal to the world who they are, or who they would like to be. Purses have very strong multi-cultural and multi-generational identification value. During this experiential, purses are decorated inside and out to represent the internal and external qualities of self.

The contents of purses are as diverse as the women who own one. The items that a woman carries in her purse are representations of the woman as a *whole*. They are symbols of who she is, and what she needs on her life journey.

Objectives

- Women select a purse that they identify with.

- Introduce the relaxation and guided imagery exercise as an example of a mindfulness practice: promote awareness of thoughts, feelings and sensations in each moment. The relaxation and guided imagery process helps to prepare participants for the management of feelings that may arise when working with an object (purse) associated with nostalgia. The multi-sensory exploration of purses from memory, as well as actual selected purses, promotes the creative and comprehensive development of a purse that represents *self*. We are better able to re-create what is familiar to us.

- Utilize guided imagery to initiate memories of purses from childhood as well as the women who carried the purses. This process increases associations of the purse and its contents with internal and external aspects of the woman who carries the purse.

- Establish a group setting to practice exploration and discussion of women in a broad context. Participants discuss their reasons for selecting their purse. Women from the past are acknowledged and honored. They are recognized and valued beyond physical attributes. Diversity and complexity are celebrated. Encourage the exploration and discussion of *metaphoric representations* of self that are carried in each participant's purse. Identify and work through the sense of vulnerability when sharing a personal aspect of self.

- Art experiential to develop a purse and its contents as a *representation of self*. Objects are created to go inside of the purse. These *metaphoric objects* represent physical, intellectual, emotional, creative or spiritual aspects of self. Qualities perceived as positive and negative are explored.

Settings
SELECTION OF PURSES
Participants choose from vintage purses that have been placed around the room. Arranging the purses so that women can see them as they enter the room promotes familiarity and comfort with the purses.

RELAXATION AND GUIDED IMAGERY
Provide a quiet space where participants can be seated or lie down while engaging in the relaxation and guided imagery process. Offer adjusted light if possible. Consider placing a "Do not disturb" sign on the door to avoid interruptions. A music player is required if you decide to incorporate music into the process.

Dialogue and Reflection

Place chairs or mats in a circular formation so that group members are able to see each other while processing.

Art Process

Participants will need adequate table space to develop their purses. Provide a separate, long table for art materials. Two or more tables may be required, depending on the amount of art materials offered, as well as the size of the group.

- Art materials: The facilitator can provide purses that have been donated or purchased from thrift stores or garage sales. Participants can also bring their own purses to develop. Art materials may include (but are not limited to): glue, glue guns, paints, markers, gold and silver paint pens, colored and decorative papers, glitter or glitter glue, beads, shells, ribbons and strings, tissue, cloth and found objects. Women may also bring items or supplies from home.

Relaxation and Guided Imagery Process

[Speak at a slow pace and allow for frequent pauses.]

Sitting on a chair or on the floor, find a position that feels comfortable and close your eyes. If you are not comfortable closing your eyes, then focus on the purse that you selected. Notice your breath as it moves in and out of your body. Feel light and comfortable. [longer pause] You are ready to transition into the world of imagination, the home of the mind's eye. Feel yourself present in the moment, open to thoughts, ideas, feelings and memories that may come forward. Anything that comes into your consciousness is allowed to move, to flow through your body as you exhale. [longer pause]

Take a few moments to think about purses from your past, purses that you remember seeing when you were a child. [pause] Do you recall purses that your mother, grandmother, aunt or caregiver carried? Picture a woman that you remember from your childhood. [longer pause] This woman may have been a family member, a friend or maybe someone less familiar, like a neighbor that you saw occasionally. Once you have established a vision of this woman, try to picture the purse that she carried. If you cannot recall an actual purse, then allow your imagination to create a purse that you sense she would have carried. [pause] The blend of memory with imagination will guide you as you take a closer look at the woman who belongs with the purse. See if you can capture the "essence" of the woman by how she carries herself, how she walks through the world. [pause]

Once visible in your mind's eye, notice the colors and textures of the purse. Imagine how it would feel to run your fingers over the surface of the purse. [pause] What is the size of the purse? Is it a small purse that carries necessary belongings efficiently; or is it a larger bag that can hold items added throughout the day? [pause] Imagine that you are able to lift the purse into the air—does the purse make any sounds, like the swooshing of material or clinking of objects inside? You are able to look inside of the purse to view the interior. Does the inside mirror the outside of the purse, or do you see new colors and textures? What objects are held within the purse? Take a few moments to imagine the items that are held by the purse. [pause] What about the smell of the purse itself? Does the bag smell like leather, or cloth, or plastic? Are there any scents coming from the inside of the purse? Do you smell lotions, perfume or cosmetic items? Do you see anything inside of the purse that has a taste, like mints, gum or candy?

Now consider the purse as a whole. Do the purse and the items inside tell you anything about the woman who carried it? Think of how she walked through the world, carrying her bag. [pause] How does her purse reflect strengths and vulnerabilities, interests and responsibilities, personality and temperament? Does her purse imply financial position, or social status? What do her purse and its contents say about family, friends and other relationships? [longer pause]

When you are ready, open your eyes and become present in the room, aware of the purse that you selected today. Examine it carefully. Consider: What is the shape of your purse? Are the lines that form your purse curvy, linear or a combination of both? What color is your purse? Does it seem that the color has faded with time? Is your purse shiny, or dull? Does it have a patina? What is attached to, or part of, your purse? Does it have zippers, or clasps? Are there pockets or compartments on the outside of the purse? How old (or young) does your purse appear to be? Move your purse around. Turn it upside down and lay it on its sides. Does your purse change shape at all when you move it? Do you notice any sounds the purse makes as it is lifted and carried? Does the purse itself have a scent like leather or cloth? Open your purse and look inside. Notice the colors, textures and composition within. Become more familiar with your purse by sketching it.

Dialogue and Reflection Process 1

Move into a group setting for dialogue/discussion of the process so far. Women are invited to share thoughts and feelings about selection of their purse; recall of purses from childhood during the relaxation and guided imagery process; memories of women who carried the purses; and the multi-sensory experience of the purses.

Participants are invited to share an object from the purses they carried to the workshop today.

Some questions to consider:

- Looking down the road into the future, what would a woman conclude about you, based on this item that you are sharing today?

- What would you like to say about the object that you are sharing? (I keep this very broad so there are no limitations on what a woman may consider or say about the object.)

- What is your attachment to the object, and what would it mean to lose the object?

- Who else knows that you carry this object, and what it means to you?

- If someone found the object that you are sharing, what might they think about the person (you) who carries it?

Art Process

1. Use a variety of materials to create a purse that reflects who you are. Without judgement, consider all aspects of self. Incorporate qualities that you consider "positive" and "negative." The inside of the purse reflects internal qualities of the self; the outside of the purse reflects qualities of the self that are shown to the world.

2. Again, use a variety of art materials to create objects to go inside of your purse. Objects can represent physical, intellectual, emotional, creative and spiritual aspects of self. These items reflect thoughts, feelings, desires and needs. Some aspects of self may be embraced, and some may be rejected. It is important to acknowledge and explore all qualities of self in this process. Examples:

- Wallet: May represent desire for financial independence and also may serve as a reminder of how financial difficulties help to shape determination and outlook on life.

- Brush and comb: May represent a familiar form of daily self-care and also may initiate thoughts and feelings about physical qualities of self that we embrace or reject.

- Calendar: May represent our desire to keep order and structure in our lives which can lead to comfort, as well as frustration when we do not meet our own expectations.

Once you have completed the art experientials, proceed to the process questions. These are discussed in a group format.

Dialogue and Reflection Process 2

Possible questions for discussion:

- What attracted you to the purse that you chose?

- Did it seem like an out on the town purse, a work purse or another type of purse?

- Were you able to develop the purse as a representation of yourself?

- What did you create to put inside of the purse, and why?

- Were there aspects that seemed easier, or more difficult, to depict or develop?

- How do you feel, looking at the purse now?

- Was there anything that you discovered about yourself in this process?

Homework

Continue to create items to go inside of your purse, based on daily events, memories of past events, hopes, dreams, even fears of the future, and thoughts and feelings about yourself and your life. Try to incorporate that which you accept about yourself and your life, as well as what you reject about yourself and your life. Remind yourself that you can examine without judgement, and are able to challenge yourself in a positive way. When bringing everything out into the light for examination, we are no longer bound by the things that we fear most about ourselves. We are able to weave a beautiful tapestry from the many parts of ourselves. We carry these parts of ourselves in our purses—they can be brought out at times to serve as reminders of who we truly are.

A Woman's Purse

Artist's Statement

A woman's purse becomes an extension of herself. The purse goes where she goes. It becomes well travelled and the inside reveals her past, present and future.

Creatively my purse took me on my own personal journey. As I held onto the handle I began to realize how I hold it to protect it and the personal stuff it has inside. Much like the way I keep some of my thoughts and feelings inside the purse and protect them as well.

I begin to look closer inside of the purse and realize that on any given day someone could open it if I allowed and all "my stuff" would be revealed. You could see old music stubs, dinner receipts, my current financial status, a photo ID and future appointments I have made.

Our lives are so busy and our purse fills up. It is full of "stuff" and it sometimes gets hard to find things. See beyond the old wrappers, papers, etc. I realize I need to clean it out. We do this in our lives too. Every once in awhile we need to clean the messes we made. Once we do, it makes our everyday lives run more smoothly. We seem happier.

Our purse is an extension of ourselves. It is our past, present and future.

Figure 6.1 My clutch

Figure 6.2 My clutch (other side)

Figure 6.3 To have and to hold

Figure 6.4 My life as a purse

7

If the Shoe Fits

Footwear for the Life Journey

INTRODUCTION

The shoe, in its simplest form, is a protective covering worn by women to promote safety and comfort of the feet. Shoes are a functional part of our everyday lives; they take us through miles of developmental stages. Shoes accompany us as we take our first steps; they can be with us as part of the burial process when the life journey comes to an end. In some ways, shoes are amongst our closest companions. Each morning when we wake up and prepare to take steps out into the world, we consider which shoes will take us where we need to go.

Shoes have a practical purpose, and they also tell the world something about who we are, or who we dream of becoming. A type of transformation occurs as we place shoes upon our feet and set out to see what the day or night will bring. In the process of removing our shoes, wiggling our toes and moving about with our feet released from confinement, we are temporarily free from the actual and symbolic definition of self. Yet we choose to return to the process of selecting and wearing shoes each day.

Shoes are familiar objects, with significant projective qualities. Exploration of shoes in the creative process brings a greater awareness and understanding of our physical, emotional, cognitive and spiritual selves. Perhaps our quest to understand a person on a deeper level by "walking a mile in her shoes" should begin with a walk in our own shoes.

Shoes have practical application in their ability to provide warmth, protection and comfort to the feet. The human foot is a complicated structure made up of bones, muscles, joints and connective tissue. The foot holds sensitive nerves that travel through the body, part of an interactive system that affects overall health. We rely upon our feet to bear weight, provide balance and move us from one place to another. Women commonly neglect their feet and force them to work beyond states of pain and fatigue. Women dance the night away, play sports, work in standing professions, chase kids and run errands for aging parents after a long day of work. As women face an accumulation of stress from domestic and/or work environments, they may retreat to salons that provide the comfort of soaking tubs and healing hands. The benefits of pedicures extend beyond the satisfaction of painted toenails; warm water and massage help reduce inflammation and increase blood flow. As women enjoy a longer life expectancy, they are giving greater consideration to physical sources of mobility. During their life journeys, their feet carry them along chosen paths. The shoes worn by females affect the overall health of feet, and by connection to her legs and hips they affect the overall function and movement of the body.

A woman requires a variety of foot coverings throughout her lifetime. The type of shoe worn at a given time may be determined by desire and/or circumstance. Shoes are often introduced at an early age in life: soft shoes or bootees may be placed on a newborn shortly after birth. These first shoes serve a practical purpose in providing warmth; however, they may also bear designs related to the caregiver's goals, desires and/or interests. As a child develops, she learns that shoes are not only functional objects that help her to move through life; they are also important accessories that reflect actual, imagined or desired identity.

Shoes are worn by a toddler as she pulls herself up, stands and walks her first steps without assistance. The shoes reveal structure as she explores the world beyond the arms of her caregivers. These first shoes are often practical in material and design. Women often recall the shape and color of their first walking shoes, as well as the smooth material that fit comfortably on their feet. The smell of white shoe polish, used to cover imperfections, frequently accompanies the memory of those shoes. A child's first shoes may offer hints about her personality. The worn and scuffed first walking shoe suggests an adventurous personality, possibly a child who takes some risks when exploring the world around her. Although the necessity of wearing shoes in the early stages of standing and walking is arguable, first walking shoes retain their status as trophies of developmental achievement. These shoes are considered to be so important that they are often preserved in bronze, pewter and lacquer coatings.

Once a child reaches kindergarten, she has some idea of whom and what she identifies with. When selecting a shoe she will likely have preference for particular colors, themes, familiar characters and textures of fabric. As she prepares to go out into the world each day, she may choose shoes that match her outfit, or she may seek contrast in her ensemble. Her shoes begin to reflect her interests and abilities. She incorporates shoes into her dress-up fantasy play. She may stroll through the house, wearing plastic high heels, pretending that she is in her kingdom, surrounded by loyal subjects. When she slips her feet into her father's boots, she is transformed into a cowgirl, running through the house to round up cattle with her pretend lasso. Once she places her mother's cozy, warm bedroom slippers upon her feet, she becomes a grown-up woman, a mother and caregiver for her dolls and animals. She imitates her mother, as well as other women who have captured her interest. The shoes she will try on as she continues to develop represent roles and relationships that she observes and/or experiences.

Types of shoes worn during the teen years are as diverse as the girls who wear them. The shoes are representations of unique qualities of self, as well as identification with groups or ideals. Shoes are accessories that reflect physical, cognitive and emotional changes taking place during this important developmental phase. A teen girl who may once have preferred a canvas sneaker may now be drawn to the fashionista stiletto (or vice versa). The iconic high heel is a symbol of transcendence into a world where sexual desire exists and romantic love is possible. Artists, musicians or independent thinkers may wear athletic shoes manufactured by a company that made the same shoes for their great grandfathers' generation. Amateur artists are called upon to paint designs on their friends' canvas sneakers. Simple images may represent complex issues: ribbons; flags; rainbows; military, religious and corporate insignias and ethnic emblems. During adolescence, a girl strengthens her sense of personal identity through the creative expression of her alliance with social causes, and connection to like-minded people.

It seems that adolescent shoe designs cross over significantly into the adult market. The road of life may have been bumpy during adolescence; but it was a road bustling with new people, opportunities, ideas, sexuality and emotions. This time that some consider the renaissance of a woman's life may be consciously or unconsciously revisited for decades to come. For some women, the shoes that she wears may reflect her desire to feel fully alive, as she did in days gone by. Other women embrace shoes that reflect wisdom, maturity and adult responsibilities. One woman in a workshop expressed her excitement that Mary Jane shoes had come back into style—a style she had worn as a young girl, and associated with her role in her family of origin. She also clarified that she wore other types of shoes when going out with friends, or hiking outdoors.

During workshops, women recall numerous reasons for wearing specific types of shoes at different times in their lives. Practical factors such as budget and product reliability may affect their choice of shoes. A woman's desire for improved self-esteem and a specific projected image may also play a role in her selection of shoes.

After facilitating dozens of shoe workshops, I no longer make assumptions about *why* a woman chooses a particular pair of shoes. Articles and advertisements in the media reflect cultural situations or trends represented in the shoes worn by women. The significant variations in the appearance and purpose of shoes may be seen in the juxtaposition of iconic images—for example, the weary young woman, wearing worn and primitive shoes as she walks along a village road, and the smiling female pop star, standing tall in shoes that lift her high above the ground for her adoring fans to see. In each case, the shoes serve a functional purpose, while helping to tell a story about the woman wearing the shoes. The shoes are representations of actual and imagined life experiences; they reflect the harsh realities of the life that one woman faces; and the illusion of a powerful life that the other woman desires. Women who attend the shoe experiential workshop have witnessed the use of shoes to tell a story; they use this awareness to bring their own unique stories to life as they develop shoes in the creative process.

The experiential workshop begins with a broad discussion of shoes and the role they have played in the lives of women. Women remember shoes that they had, or wanted to have. They recall shoes worn at different times in their lives, for different reasons. These shoes are often associated with relationships, situations and roles in life. The connection to shoes as familiar objects with nostalgic connotation brings depth and richness to emotional responses, which range from gentle laughter to profound sadness and grief.

Following the group discussion, women are encouraged to choose one shoe from a wide variety of shoes set out around the room. The shoes may be shaped from very basic patterns and fabrics; they may also be fashioned from extraordinary designs and materials. I try to include a broad range of shoes: dressy, classy, sexy, boyish, athletic, conservative, artistic, old-fashioned and outdated. I include shoes that are brand new and shoes that are well worn. Participants have provided feedback that my brief explanation that the shoes have been treated with disinfectant spray helps to reduce anxiety in the selection of shoes. With this awareness, women seem to consider all of the shoes, even those that show more wear and tear.

Once each woman has selected her shoe and is seated at her workspace, I provide the directive: "Bring your shoe to life as a representation of yourself. Consider all aspects of yourself: the physical, cognitive, emotional and spiritual parts of who you are." I encourage the women to allow their imagination to flow, and to give the art some of the control in the process. Because the final project may be difficult to conceptualize, I provide examples of two very different, completed shoes. One is a more symbolic representation of self, with colors and shapes that allude to physical form and personality but do not portray them literally. The other shoe has hair, eyelashes, glasses, a mouth, ears, breasts, hips, a dress and jewelry. These sample shoes are intended as a very general frame of reference. I stress that anything is possible in this creative process. The wide variety of art materials promotes the opportunity to express individuality and create unique qualities with each shoe.

We cannot truly know what it is like to walk in another person's shoes, unless we understand the deeper, symbolic nature of shoes themselves. A woman's shoes protect her feet as she travels along the road of life. As steady companions, they move her over the smooth and bumpy patches she encounters along the way. A woman's shoes become familiar with her personality; her thoughts, feelings, beliefs and behaviors. They help to project an image of who she is, or who she would like to become. Shoes serve as holding vessels for the woman's feet; her feet are in constant communication with the rest of her body. The shoes bear witness to how the woman relates to her body, and how that perception of her body affects the way she walks in the world. Seeing the world from the ground floor up, they take everything into consideration when telling the story.

Once a shoe takes on the symbolic, physical form of a woman in the creative process, she sees herself from a unique perspective, with the eyes of an artist. A woman's shoes, her close companions, tell the broader story of what it is like for her to walk that mile stretch of road.

EXPERIENTIAL

Theme

A woman's walk through life is a physical journey as well as a symbolic one. In Chapter 6 we explored the value of a purse as a functional accessory to assist a woman in her travels; in this chapter we examine shoes in a similar way. Shoes are familiar, constant objects that mirror back qualities of self from a unique perspective. Shoes represent a grounding of the physical body to connect with the earth and Mother Nature. They provide stability and promote opportunity for adventure along the road of life. Shoes, diverse in appearance and symbolism, become the means for each woman to tell her story. In this creative process, women bring all aspects of self to life in the creative development of a chosen shoe. Each woman is supported in taking a non-judgemental stance to explore how she perceives herself as she walks along the road of life.

Metaphors

As women walk along the road of life, shoes help to absorb the shock of the road and protect the feet from harmful surfaces and objects encountered on the way. A woman's shoes may reference her life situation: her socio-economic status, ideals and causes she embraces, her strengths and limitations and her developmental stage of life (actual or imagined). Shoes, like the iconic slippers in the stories of Cinderella and Dorothy in "The Wizard of Oz," may represent *transformation* from one age or life stage to another. Shoes are projective objects that promote expression of thoughts, ideas and emotions related to the conceptualization of self. Shoes tell the story of the woman that they carry along the road of life. They are the holders of her life experiences, and containers of hopes and dreams for the future. In this experiential, participants choose a shoe to accompany them on the road to self-discovery.

Objectives

- Reinforce relaxation as an example of mindfulness practice: practice deep breathing and progressive muscle relaxation. Promote non-judgemental exploration of thoughts, feelings and sensations in the moment.

- Group discussion to discuss the personal and societal relevance of shoes. This may include: historical significance, developmental implications, associations with roles and relationships, language references to shoes (e.g. "fill her shoes," "walk all over you"), diversity of shape and materials of shoes.

- Explore the metaphoric relevance of shoes specifically related to body image. Discuss the relationship between the shoes that a woman chooses to wear, and her perception of her physical body. How do the shoes she is wearing today bear witness to her body image? (Continue to address the vulnerability when sharing personal aspects of self.)

- Art experiential to develop a shoe as a representation of self: physical, emotional, cognitive and relational.

Settings

SELECTION OF SHOES

Participants choose from a variety of shoes that have been placed around the room. As with the purses in the previous chapter, placing the shoes so that they are visible when women enter the room promotes familiarity and comfort with the shoes and process.

RELAXATION AND GUIDED IMAGERY

Provide a quiet space where participants can sit or lie down while practicing deep relaxation. Consider progressive muscle relaxation. If you are using floor space, mats are desirable. Offer adjusted light if possible. You will need a music player if you decide to incorporate music into the process. Consider placing a "Do not disturb" sign on the door to avoid interruptions.

DIALOGUE AND REFLECTION
Provide a space where participants can sit in a circle for a group discussion. Again, if you are using floor space, mats are desirable. If you have chairs, arrange them in a circle. (Do ahead of time if possible.)

ART PROCESS
Participants will need adequate work space to develop their shoes. Provide at least one separate table for art materials. (Participants should be able to walk around the table to explore materials.) Two or more tables may be required, depending on the variety of art materials and size of the group.

• Art materials: Facilitator provides shoes that have been donated or purchased at thrift stores or garage sales. To *prepare the shoes*, place them on newspaper and spray inside and out with disinfectant spray. Participants may also bring their own shoes; however, they would need to understand the directive ahead of time in order to select the right shoe. Art materials may include (but are not limited to): glue, glue guns, paints, markers, gold and silver paint pens, colored and decorative papers, glitter or glitter glue, beads, shells, ribbons and strings, tissue, cloth, found objects, moveable eyes, eyeglasses and sunglasses. Women may bring personal objects from home.

Relaxation and Guided Imagery Process

[Speak at a slow pace and allow frequent pauses.]

Sitting on a chair, or on the floor, find a position that feels comfortable. Close your eyes if you feel comfortable doing so. If not, focus your eyes on an area or object in the room—your eyes should feel comfortable, relaxed. Begin to notice your breath as it moves in and out of your body. [pause] Become aware of yourself breathing. [pause] Feel yourself becoming relaxed and comfortable.

Move your attention to your feet. [pause] Focus for a moment on your toes. [pause] Wiggle your toes. Gently tighten the muscles in your toes and hold for a moment. [pause] Relax the muscles in your toes. [pause] Now gently tense the muscles in your feet and hold for a moment. [pause] Now relax the muscles in your feet. [pause] Remember to breathe in and out. [pause] As you exhale, you release all of the tension held in your feet. In this moment, your feet may be completely at rest, filled with warmth and lightness.

Continue to feel yourself breathing. [pause] You are aware of your breath, moving in and out. [pause] Become aware of your calves. [pause] Gently tighten the muscles in your calves. [pause] Now relax the muscles and allow your calves to be at rest. [pause] Continue to breathe in slowly. [pause] As you breathe out, you release the tension from your calves. [pause]

Focus your attention on your thighs. [pause] Gently tighten the muscles in your thighs. [pause] Relax the muscles in your thighs and allow them to be at rest. [pause] Continue to breathe in slowly. [pause] As you breathe out, you release the tension held in your thighs.

With your mind's eye, move upward in your body. Focus your awareness on your hips and buttocks. [pause] Gently tighten the muscles in that area. [pause] Relax the muscles, allowing your hips and buttocks to be at rest. [pause] Continue to breathe in and out, slowly. [pause] As you breathe out, release any tension held in your lower body. [pause]

Now focus your awareness on your stomach, a place where stress and tension are often held. [pause] Remember to breathe in and out, slowly. Gently tighten your stomach muscles. [pause] Now relax the muscles. [pause] Feel the tension move away from your stomach as you breathe out, slowly. [pause]

Focus your attention on your lower back. [pause] Gently tighten the muscles in your lower back. [pause] Relax the muscles, allowing your lower back to be at rest. Feel yourself breathing, slowly and deeply. [pause] Breathe away the tension you hold in your lower back. [pause] Feel the lightness in your back and lower body. [pause]

Focus your awareness on your chest. [pause] Gently tighten the muscles in your chest. [pause] Relax the muscles, and allow your chest to be at rest. [pause] Remember to breathe in and out, releasing the tension from the chest area. [pause]

Move your attention to your shoulders and neck—parts of your body that carry the weight of worry throughout the day. Gently tighten the muscles in that area. [pause] Now relax the muscles.

[pause] Breathe in deeply. [pause] As you exhale, release the tension and feel the lightness in your neck and shoulders. [pause]

Focus on your upper arms and elbows. [pause] Continue to breathe in and out, slowly and deeply. [pause] Gently tighten the muscles in your upper arms and elbows. [pause] Breathe out as you release the tension. [pause] Feel your arms and elbows at rest.

Pay attention to your lower arms, wrists, hands and fingers. [pause] Gently tighten the muscles in those areas. [pause] Release the tension, and relax the muscles. [pause] Feel the lightness in your hands and arms. [pause]

Move your attention to your head and face. [pause] Continue to breathe, slowly and deeply. Gently tighten all of the muscles in your head and face. Feel the muscles relax around your jaw; [pause] your cheeks; [pause] your eyes and mouth. [pause] Tighten the muscles on your forehead, and around your head. [pause] Relax those muscles, allowing your head and face to be at rest. [pause]

Breathe slowly and deeply. [pause] As you exhale, feel any remaining tension move away. Your muscles are in a restful, relaxed state. [pause]

You are aware of yourself, in the room, on the chair (or floor), in this moment of time. [pause]

There is no need to worry about yesterday or tomorrow; this is the moment that matters. [pause]

You allow thoughts and feelings to flow through your mind and body with ease. [pause] You are prepared to look at yourself without judgement. On this day you see yourself with the eyes of an artist.

You are ready to open the doors to the imagination, and allow creative energy to flow through. [pause]

When you are ready, open your eyes and be present in the room.

Move to the circle for group discussion.

Dialogue and Reflection Process 1

Possible topics and questions for discussion:

- Consider the purpose/meaning of shoes in a cultural context.
- Discuss the diversity of shoes. Relate it to the diversity of women.

- Why do we wear shoes? What is it like to go barefoot?

- What type of shoes did you wear at different ages of your life? Did you choose the shoes, or did someone choose them for you?

- As a child, did you observe shoes that other people wore?

- Were there any shoes that you wanted, but couldn't have?

- Consider different roles that you have in your life: what type of shoes do you wear in those roles?

- Are the types of shoes that you select to wear affected by any relationships in your life?

- What are some famous stories about shoes? How do you relate to those stories?

- Do you ever select shoes in response to your body image?

- Do the shoes that you wear ever have an effect on how you feel about your body on a given day or night?

- If you were a shoe, what type of shoe would you be?

- Describe yourself, as that shoe, walking along the road of life.

Art Process

The relaxation process helps participants relax and take a mindful, non-judgemental approach to the creative exploration of self. The group discussion of shoes promotes a broad consideration of the meaning of shoes, culturally and personally. Women are encouraged to tap into the world of imagination to explore shoes as representations of self.

> Take some time to examine the shoes positioned around the room. You are looking for a shoe to represent who you are in the world: physically, emotionally, intellectually and spiritually, as well as any other parts of self. Pay particular attention to any shoes that you are immediately drawn to. You may pick the shoes up for a closer look. Place the shoes down by your feet; hold them in front of you. You may want to walk away from shoes that capture your interest in order to see it/them from another perspective. Once you feel satisfied that you have found your shoe, you may take it to your workspace.

> Develop your shoe as a representation of who you are in the world. Consider all qualities of self.
>
> [Show examples of finished shoes.]

Dialogue and Reflection Process 2

Possible questions for discussion:

- How are you feeling?

- Did you feel resistance at any point in the process? How did you overcome those feelings?

- Were you able to stay present in the moment, during the art process? What was that like?

- Describe the process of selecting a shoe to represent who you are in the world.

- Tell us about your shoe.

- What thoughts, feelings and memories does your shoe hold for you?

- What does your shoe say about your travels together along the road of life?

- Did you discover anything about yourself in this process?

Homework

> Place your shoe in a visible location. Imagine a life adventure you might take while wearing this shoe. What are the physical qualities of the shoe that you recognize and appreciate? What other qualities does the shoe reflect that you identify with? Let your shoe continue to walk you on the road of self-discovery.

If the Shoe Fits

Artist's Statement

We are all destined to grow old. This shoe reminds us to age gracefully, with loving kindness, gratitude and with an acceptance of the limitations and imperfections that present themselves as we age.

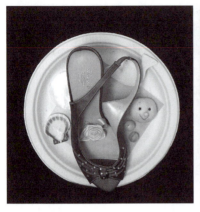

Figure 7.1 "This is me"

Figure 7.2 Silk wings and other things

Figure 7.3 Destination Grandma

8

Beyond Skin Deep

Barbie Finds Her Voice

INTRODUCTION

As we travel along this journey we call life, we've all encountered a Barbie doll along the way. Barbie's debut into the American market in 1959 marked the beginning of her own journey and she would influence the lives of Western girls for decades to come. Women passionately argue the pros and cons of Barbie's very existence; yet everyone seems to agree the plastic doll has made a significant impression on the collective minds of young girls in the West. She is an icon, and arguably a modern archetypal representation of ideal female beauty. One has only to Google "Barbie" to see over a million sites referencing every possible aspect of her being. We may never be able to precisely measure the impact she's had on the female psyche. What is known with certainty, however, is that 50 years after her creation Barbie maintains an influential presence in the Western female mind.

The latter half of the twentieth century bore witness to significant advancements in women's rights, as expectations and regulations related to work, education and family planning continued to evolve. The second wave of the feminist movement paved the roads of opportunity for women to explore a world once dominated by men. Although Barbie took on many jobs and responsibilities that were described as progressive, she consistently maintained a body type considered by many to be stereotypical, unrealistic and unhealthy. That premise is supported by a study at the University Central Hospital in Finland: researchers found that Barbie is too thin. They concluded that if she were a living, breathing woman she would not have the necessary amount of fat on her body to be able to menstruate (cited in Winterman, 2009).

Barbie's identities are representative of popular cultural trends. Mattel (the creators of Barbie) responded to the changing roles of women by altering Barbie's hair, make-up, skin color, clothing and accessories, to reflect her inclusion in the changing roles—she has been associated with numerous and diverse occupations throughout her history. We have seen her depicted as a rock star, a movie star, a model and a designer. She has taken on jobs in the helping professions, such as nursing, teaching, law enforcement and fire fighting. She has been a pilot, a doctor and a paleontologist. The list of Barbie's professions is as numerous and diverse as the women she has endeavored to represent.

Barbie's body shape has always been more consistent with that of a fashion model than that of an average woman in most sectors of the workforce. She is promoted as a woman able to tackle any job or responsibility while maintaining a sense of style and beauty. In 1965, several years before women actually entered the space program, Mattel introduced Astronaut Barbie to the world of girls who wanted to grow up and have challenging and interesting jobs. Three years after Astronaut Barbie was introduced, and in the same year that feminists proclaimed that "sisterhood is powerful," Barbie spoke her first words. With the simple pull of a string, she proclaimed: "I have a date tonight" and "I love being a fashion model." Sadly, the content of her messages seemed to align with the stereotype of her body and her beauty, and not with her development as a woman making strides in advancement towards equality.

In fairness to Barbie, she didn't sign up to be the feminist role model that some hoped she would become. One of her strengths has always been her ability to help girls create and develop a variety of personas during imaginary play. The roles and personalities that one Barbie doll can take on in the hands of a creative girl has no limits. Still, it's obvious that she is not a baby doll to be taken care of, but an adult woman who girls can aspire to be like. For this reason she is unique, even as she stands on the shelves beside her imitators and competitors.

The concept of a workshop developing Barbie dolls grew from a meeting with a group of women gathered to brainstorm ideas for art workshops. We were looking for projects that women of all ages could relate to. During the meeting our attention shifted to several pairs of long white gloves that had been donated for art projects. We imagined that the gloves, lying casually on the table, had been placed there by the women who had worn them. They seemed to come to life as we slipped our hands into them. We recalled images of women who were photographed wearing opera-style gloves to balls and other formal affairs. Images of two women were particularly vivid: Jacqueline Kennedy and Barbie (so include images of Jackie and Barbie).

A buzz of questions filled the room as the women wondered aloud *why* women wore the long white gloves, and how they felt about wearing them. Did the women enjoy wearing the gloves because they added a touch of elegance to their ensemble? Did they feel pressure or obligation to wear them as a sign of modesty, virtue or social status? The group fantasized about what it would be like to have a living, breathing Barbie available to share her thoughts and feelings about wearing the gloves. This led to speculations about what Barbie might say about other things. What would she have to say about the jobs she had been associated with? How did she feel about her relationship with Ken and how they had been portrayed as a couple? In her 50 years of existence, what changes had she seen taking place in the world, and how did she perceive the women of yesterday and today? We decided that an art workshop that would give voice to Barbie would be fun to explore.

I began to hunt for Barbie dolls at garage sales and thrift stores. I asked friends and family members if they would like to donate dolls to the project. It didn't take long to gather a small collection of dolls that would be used in the first "Barbie Speaks" experiential. Two women signed up to be part of the first art workshop. Based on an initial group discussion, the women decided to withhold judgement on Barbie's stereotypical, unrealistic beauty. They would look beyond the clever marketing schemes that had been used to promote Barbie, and experience her as a woman with heart and soul. She would be given a symbolic voice to express her views of her world and the world around her. The significance of Barbie's message would be based on the pretense that her words were her own, not the product of the women's own projections. The irony, of course, is that in this process the women were able to reap the benefits of what Barbie does best: promote imaginary play.

At the beginning of the workshop, various dolls were placed in the middle of a table and the women were encouraged to select one that they wanted to work with. One young woman, who will be called Laura, selected a Barbie "wannabe" from the group of dolls. The doll she selected appeared to be the type that had been sold at gas stations in the 70s—one of many in a world collection. The doll was much shorter than Barbie, with a body size and shape like that of a pre-pubescent young woman. Her clothes, stapled to her plastic frame, were clearly outdated. Laura expressed a sense of connection to this doll. She also selected an actual Barbie doll from the collection, and said that she would like to work with both. Another young lady in my group, who will be called Alex, selected a classic Barbie wearing a minimal amount of clothing. Alex turned the Barbie around, noticing the smoothness of her skin. She contemplated what it would be like to depict Barbie in a contemporary fashion, in a way that she had never been viewed before.

Laura developed her "Barbie wannabe" by placing a gown designed for a Barbie doll on her short body. She cut some hair off of the head of the Barbie doll and glued it onto the wannabe doll. Then she glued the head of the Barbie onto the chest of the wannabe, to look like it was being held by the "jealous" doll. She attached one of Barbie's arms and one of her legs to the other doll's body. The leg stuck out below the hem of the dress, and the arm held on to Barbie's head. The image of the two dolls blended together was described by Laura as "kind of freaky." She described the wannabe doll as taking on characteristics of Barbie out of a desire to be like her. In order for the wannabe doll to try to look like Barbie, she had to wear hair and clothes that really didn't fit her style and personality. The adaptation reflected an attempt to meet the cultural stereotypes of beauty at any cost, even the sacrifice of self.

Alex carefully painted a tattoo of a shark on the arm of the Barbie she had selected. She wondered out loud what it meant for women to modify themselves with different forms of body art. Alex pulled her Barbie's hair down over her face and secured it with a rubber band. She commented on her desire to have viewers focus on Barbie's body art, and not on her famous face. She decided to take Barbie home to experiment with temporary tattoos. She expressed excitement that she would be allowed to alter Barbie in a way that was intriguing to her, and in a fashion that she would never consider doing to herself. It was interesting to note the stages of apprehension, acceptance and freedom that both women seemed to experience and move through in the process.

As Laura and Alex continued to develop Barbie in later workshops, they became increasingly confident and vocal. Both women were able to look beyond Barbie's familiar beauty to explore her inner world, including challenges that she might face. Laura expressed sympathy concerning Barbie's confinement to the box that she is packaged in—she noted that Barbie was bound to the box in such a way that she could not possibly move. She reflected on how it must feel to be trapped or restrained. Laura eventually developed new packaging for Barbie. She used colorful paper to collage a container that could hold the doll. Five simple words stood out in bold letters on the face of the packaging: "Be not me, be you."

I continue to receive periodic feedback from the two young women who attended the first "Barbie Speaks" workshop. They continue to pose questions related to Barbie: What would her survival kit look like? What would she shop for at the grocery store? The women expressed joy and humor when exploring alternative associations with Barbie; however, Laura reminded us that stereotypical standards set by Barbie are not easily overcome:

> There is still a side of me that wants to look like Barbie in some ways. There is still a part of me that wants to be that thin. And plus she has everything my ideal life would have. She has the job, the car, the house, the vacations that I will never have. I shouldn't compare myself to a piece of plastic but I can't help myself sometimes.

Women have presented dozens of follow-up ideas for the "Barbie Speaks" workshop. The concept of what Barbie *could* be like stimulates the imagination. I have come to value the contributions that a single plastic doll can make in helping women to go beyond skin deep in search of the self. In the experiential workshops, Barbie is finding yet another role as an outspoken woman who is able to tell her audience what is on her mind. In this process, she becomes the role model that so many hoped for, after all.

EXPERIENTIAL

Theme

As we travel on the journey from childhood to adulthood, we are often accompanied by memories of people or objects that remain constant because of the impact they had on our lives. We may have had actual interactions with these people or objects, or we may have perceived them in such a way that they earned a place on the memory shelves in our minds. There are a few toys that are so constant in the lives of girls that they leave an imprint in the developing world of object relations, and have the ability to impact the perception of self in relation to family, culture and world. Barbie is a doll that women of all ages can relate to on some level. She has effectively promoted girls' projective fantasies for over five decades. She is not a blank canvas for childish projections; however, she represents a specific size, shape and image. Regardless of what a child imagines that she is, or can be, when she plays with her doll she must also face what she is not, and will not ever be. During this art process women step outside of their own sense of self-evaluation in relation to Barbie, and allow her to speak about life from her own unique perspective. Women can apply this process to examination of self on their journey of self-discovery.

Metaphors

During this art process, women connect to Barbie as they symbolically give her a voice. They help her to express a broad range of ideas and emotions. Barbie is able to proclaim thoughts and feelings related to how she has been stereotyped and potentially perceived by others over the years. Workshop participants may sense that Barbie is also a projective representation of self, and therefore the process may seem unfamiliar or uncomfortable. It is important to acknowledge that the process of exploring the qualities of self hidden beneath the mask of beauty may initiate feelings that are difficult, even painful. In a safe environment, where women feel that they will not be judged by others, they are able to explore qualities of self that may normally be avoided or rejected. Women discover more about their own thoughts, feelings and opinions as they work with Barbie to develop her voice—a voice that speaks to the experience of being a woman.

Objective

Create a safe, trusting environment that promotes some regression in childlike play while exploring and communicating aspects of self.

Setting

Provide adequate table or surface space for the development of Barbie dolls. A separate table may be provided for art materials. Set up a separate station for glue guns. A music player is required to play music during the process, if desired. Chairs placed in a circle are ideal for group dialogue and reflection.

- Art materials: Barbie dolls (dolls may be purchased at garage sales and thrift stores, and participants may also bring their own Barbies); imitation Barbie dolls; Barbie clothes, shoes and accessories if available; magazines and books to cut images, words and passages from; glue, glue guns and glitter glue; paints and markers; gold and silver pens; colored and decorative papers; beads and jewelry; shells and nature objects; ribbons and strings; tissue, cloth and fabrics. Women may also bring items or supplies from home.

Art Process

This is an opportunity to give *voice* to your Barbie doll. You can depict Barbie's voice symbolically in the art process so that she can speak to her life experiences, her life situation and life in general. She has been in the public eye for over 50 years yet we don't know how she feels about critical issues such as wars, disease, natural disasters and climate change. She has never weighed in on politics or the changing role of women in the world. This is an opportunity for Barbie to speak to the pressures she faces to remain youthful and beautiful. Has she paid a price for that beauty? What are her goals in life—are there goals that have not been met, or dreams that seem lost? What are her likes and dislikes? What would she change in her life and what would she keep the same? What would she say if she could speak? Try to look beyond her mask of beauty, to find what lies beneath.

Dialogue and Reflection Process

Describe your overall sense of this process.

- How did you relate to the dolls when you first saw them?
- How did you select your doll?

- What was it like to look beyond Barbie's stereotypical beauty to relate to her as a woman with a voice?

- Do you recall the first thing that came to mind when imagining what Barbie might have to say?

- What was your reaction to that voice?

- Were you able to express Barbie's voice in the art process?

- Can you describe how you used the art to develop her voice?

- Did you experience your own voice?

- What did you learn about yourself in this process?

Homework

Continue to develop the voice of Barbie. As you watch the evening news or read the newspaper, imagine what Barbie would say about the issues that impact our world. How are her thoughts and feelings different from, or the same as, yours? Place Barbie somewhere visible to serve as a reminder that substance and character originate *from the inside out.*

You were able to set aside judgement of Barbie based on her physical appearance while exploring who she is as a *whole* woman. You can do the same for yourself. Your ongoing journey of self-discovery will take you below skin deep to examine parts of yourself that you appreciate, as well as parts of yourself that you acknowledge and continue to work on. Just as Barbie speaks her truth, you speak your truth. Hear and appreciate your own voice.

Beyond Skin Deep

Artist's Statement

My Barbie has curlers reminiscent of the kind worn in the 1950s. She has the vulnerability and the curiosity of women of that era. She has the determination of a very strong man who is poised to take on the world. She is surrounded by different cultures. Her family watches her and the world watches her. I AM STRONG. I AM HERE.

Figure 8.1 I want to be Barbie

Figure 8.2 Let heads roll!

9

Reframe Your Frame

Celebrating the Culture of the Human Body

INTRODUCTION

Women journey near and far to explore ideas, beliefs and values in cultures that are different from their own. The female traveler is familiarized with the roles and customs of foreign women through the experience of the art, music, food and language of the land. Women are interested in the conditions in which other women live, as well as the roles that women play in developing and sustaining cultural settings. Western women look with a critical eye at the condition and treatment of women around the world, voicing compassion and demands for change when injustices are perceived.

As women look into the broader world community to explore mental and physical health issues that affect other women, the culture of body hatred and body harm taking place on the home front persists. An important aspect of the cultural climate related to body image is the derogatory self-talk that women learn at an early age. This language affirms overall negative self-evaluation, promoting an oppressive climate that slashes through the entire culture. Western women are shockingly assimilated to a culture that demands a standardized beauty, at any cost.

Women's issues, on a global scale, have become an important aspect of how the West does business with the rest of the world. Women in the West have been voting for nearly a century; they are aware of how that single process can affect other women so broadly. Women pay attention to how politicians treat their own wives and partners. They watch to see how votes are cast on issues relating to women and children. Women are interested in health challenges faced by women of the world: reproductive rights, pregnancy and childbirth, sexually transmitted infections, violence, disease and nutrition. Western women are bloggers, lobbyists, women's conference organizers, letter writers, expressive artists, complainers (to anyone who can listen and help) and role models to their own children at home and in the community. Women gain understanding about the broader world, and themselves, as they explore the culture and languages of people they meet along the road of life.

Women were born to move. The movement takes place in body, mind and spirit. There may be significant variations in the means and opportunity for actual travel; however, women are able to tap the resources of the imagination to explore and integrate different cultural experiences. Western women are introduced to women around the world through literary works that describe them, art that depicts them, and the food and language that move through the very center of their being. The internet allows for fast and easy access to information relating to the lives and plights of women beyond one nation's boundaries. Articles and blogs allow women to see what their foreign counterparts are doing in their day-to-day lives: health issues, overall political climate and the voice, or lack of voice, that women have within the culture. Women are an intrinsic part of social definition, regardless of the role that they play within the society. A deliberate minimization or exclusion of women in a cultural setting contributes to the general condition of that setting. The very absence of women signifies the importance of women within the culture.

Women are natural activists because of an innate, collective knowledge: cultural climate affects health attitudes and services, and women's overall health has an impact on the well-being of the culture. Minimization of the body hatred and body harm taking place across Western countries seems counter-intuitive to what women hold to be valuable and critical for the health of the culture. Empowered women who reach out to help women across the globe may openly or secretly participate in dangerous diets, undergo risky plastic surgery and/or engage in excessive exercise or compensatory product consumption. We have a distinct culture-within-a-culture related to expectations of body size and appearance. Deviation from standardized beauty may result in rejection or exclusion in relationships and pursuits. In a land recognized for strength of diversity, women continue to struggle under the pressure to "fit the mold."

The language that accompanies negative self-evaluation is introduced at an early age. Toddlers begin to acquire the language by mimicking words uttered by primary caregivers and other influential girls and women in their lives. Girls at this age do not fully understand the meaning of the words; however, they are familiarized with the sounds and emotions associated with the words. For instance, many young girls have an understanding of the word "fat" and are able to point to a body part that has an appearance or sensation of being large or heavy. Young girls do not understand the important role of fat in the body, or the reasons for variation in the amount of fat within each person's body. They learn that fat on the body causes women in their lives to respond emotionally when looking in the mirror, or trying on clothes. For very young girls, the word "fat" may accidentally (or intentionally) become associated with unhappiness, fear and anger. School-age girls begin to attach broader meaning to simple words and statements related to body size. At this age, the word "fat" may evoke a mental reference to something being wrong, or out of place.

As a girl moves into adolescence, the feeling that something is wrong or out of place in her body may result in a sense of disconnect from the peer group. During this critical developmental stage, the culture, driven by the advertising industry, becomes a virtual mirror that reflects back information that is used in identity formation. Teenage girls do not understand that the images reflected back from the cultural mirror are not precise. They are often deliberately distorted to cause an emotional reaction or behavioral response. The culture may try to convince a young woman that she does not look the way she should, with the intent to sell her a product or service. Teens use the cultural mirror as a weapon against each other when they deliberately point out imperfections and shortcomings in an attempt to raise their own status or sense of self. During adolescence, the language of self and relation to others is often a language that references the body. By the time a girl reaches adolescence, she has experienced the world of negative body image through the eyes of other girls and women. She has listened to the way that her father, brothers and/or other males discuss the female body. She has been bombarded with media images and messages that insist on a specific body weight and appearance. She carries all of this into an age that is hallmarked by self-doubt and desire for acceptance. The conditions have been set for how she feels about herself as she transitions into adulthood.

Women move forward into adult life cognitively equipped to challenge the culture and language that perpetuates negative body evaluation. As a woman explores her identity within the culture and broader world community, she continues to encounter messages and experiences that have the potential to influence her definition of self. Although she will have opportunities to integrate positive language and images related to self-image, she may continue to defer to thoughts and beliefs that she internalized during childhood and adolescence. This learned way of being in the world becomes systematically integrated into the thought processes of the female mind. A woman may resist the process of looking beyond what she *believes* to be true in order to explore her body in a new and profound way.

Safety and validation must be established in order for women to begin to explore the culture of body appreciation. The ideal setting is one that promotes creativity so that ideas and emotions may be expressed in spoken language and imagery. The "Reframe Your Frame" workshop encourages participants to see their bodies with the eyes of an artist, focused on creation rather than (perceived) objective observation. Discomfort and vulnerability are acknowledged as a natural part of the process; women are supported in allowing these feelings to move through mind and body as they create.

This experiential workshop begins with a relaxation and guided imagery process to continue the practice of breath awareness and mindful presence. This initial part of the experiential sets the tone for a non-judgemental awareness of the physical body as a holding vessel for the many unseen parts of self. I have noticed that women often arrive at this workshop with heightened anxiety because of the direct approach to working with actual parts of the body.

Clinicians refer participants to this group once they have reached a stage where eating disorder behaviors have been reduced and cognitive function is restored. Participants must be able to focus, think abstractly and access internal and external support beyond the safety of the workshop environment. This is not an appropriate process for women who are just beginning treatment for eating disorders, or for women who are utilizing maladaptive coping strategies. If a participant is currently in treatment for an eating disorder, then I consult with the individual therapist providing the treatment and coordination of services. I speak with participants (over the phone usually) prior to sign-up for the group. These are some questions I may ask:

- How did you hear about the group and what do you know about it?

- Are you currently receiving any type of counseling services?

- If so, is your therapist aware of your interest in this group? How would this process fit into the current goals of treatment?

- This process requires an exploration of the body using positive statements and imagery. This approach may feel unfamiliar and uncomfortable; however, other group members will experience similar feelings and we will work through that as part of the process. How does that sound to you?

During this process, participants are guided into a "foreign land" of positive self-evaluation, to experience the language and customs of that land. Anticipation of the journey can be extremely anxiety-provoking, and may initiate resistance in many forms. This is to be expected, and should be acknowledged at the beginning of the process. Women seem less fearful of the anxiety they are experiencing if they understand that this is a normal, manageable response.

Let's imagine a woman is traveling by plane to a new and strange land. She has never been on a plane before and does not know what to expect. The flight is turbulent and she is rocked up and down in her seat. She finally sets her feet on the ground; however, she remains distracted by her fearful responses during the flight. Her system may remain on high alert as she completes her travels through the land, preventing her from full participation in the experience. A seasoned traveler could have helped the woman understand common occurrences during flights (i.e. turbulence) and the likeliness of some fear or discomfort, and have introduced discussion of ways to calm the body and mind along the way: breath awareness while imaging a safe and comforting place; distraction with movies and magazines; talking with other travelers; positive affirmations ("I am safe and will be on the ground soon").

The relaxation and guided imagery process at the beginning of the workshop helps participants feel present in their body, allowing thoughts and feelings to move in, and away. They are encouraged to experience their bodies with the mind of a creator and the eyes of an artist.

The first group of women that I worked with in this process was a group that I recall when describing the challenges and potential pitfalls of the process. The group was made up of four women from diverse backgrounds. They were in various stages of body image awareness: one had been to residential treatment for an eating disorder; one was active in an eating disorder and was receiving individual therapy; one was a provider who wanted to experience the process to enhance her body image support group; another was a young woman who constantly compared her body to her mother's body, causing constant negative self-evaluation. The women had not worked together before; the setting was foreign. As each woman entered the room, I noticed a look of apprehension followed by a visual tracking associated with body comparison. There was a strange mixture of tension and excitement in the air.

As the women moved to their mats for the relaxation and guided imagery process, a sense of nervousness filled the room. It became apparent to me that some members were not going to be as comfortable as others during the breathing and relaxation process. The woman who was experiencing active eating disorder symptoms had a difficult time closing her eyes. She looked around the room during the process and did not seem to want to connect to her body on any level. Surprisingly, the woman who facilitated a body image support group also seemed to have some difficulty in the process. She made periodic, disruptive comments regarding her lack of physical comfort on the mat. She declined the chair that I offered. I quickly realized that this member, one I had hoped might provide some leadership in the group, had resistance to exploring the feeling of being present in her body. The young woman who compared herself to her mother seemed to be trying hard to do everything just right. The woman who had received residential treatment moved into the process with comfort; she had been in group settings before and meditation on a daily basis. In this case, I acknowledged the possibility of apprehension and anxiety after the fact.

This initial group provided valuable information: safety and validation are critical aspects of the cultural setting. Participants should have a sense of the culture when they enter the room. Soft, instrumental background music and low lighting (or candles) help to create a relaxing environment. Participants are engaged in light conversation upon arrival; I have placed humorous or inspirational quotes from well-known women on the table to facilitate conversation. Members are encouraged to find a comfortable position on the mats or chairs, and we discuss the possibility that many types of thoughts and feelings may come to conscious awareness in the process. Resistance is explored as the mind's way to defend against the perceived threat of anxiety; techniques to help tension and stress are introduced. The cultural landscape is designed so that each group member is able to benefit from the process, even if she is not able to participate fully. For example, an object in the room serves as a visual focal point for women who do not want to close their eyes. The ability to focus on any part of the body, or function taking place in the body, may be particularly difficult for a woman who consciously avoids thoughts of her body. If participants are not able to concentrate fully on the breathing process, they are encouraged to try to establish some presence while allowing the flow of air to move through the body.

I encourage women to explore art supplies in the room before moving to the tables to begin the experiential. Materials and music that are unexpected and fun lighten the atmosphere and introduce the culture of creativity. Humor and laughter sprinkled throughout the process help to soothe anxious minds and calm systems that are on "accidental" high alert. As a woman eases into practices associated with the culture of positive self-evaluation, she experiences herself in a new way. Her heart, mind and spirit become lighter, brighter and open to new possibilities.

EXPERIENTIAL

Theme

As a woman travels the road of her life, she discovers new worlds beyond her horizon. Some places in her journey may appear very different from what she was accustomed to in her native land. In the lands she explores, she encounters novel customs, strange languages and dress, and varied roles for her gender. When a woman arrives in a foreign land, she may join with fellow travelers to fully experience a new way of being in the world. Her role as an explorer encompasses discoveries in the environments that surround her, as well as in the worlds of her body, mind and spirit. She experiences life from a new perspective, and her frames of reference associated with who she is in the world are forever altered. As she experiences the newness of the world around her, she also experiences the newness of herself.

This experiential prepares participants for an incredible journey into a distant, foreign land. Initially, the land may be perceived as fraught with dangers. In order to reduce a woman's sense of vulnerability, she is given supplies to carry with her: validation, affirmations, a non-judgemental awareness of self and a sense of connection to other women.

Metaphors

Creative exploration of specific parts of the body can be an especially challenging process for many women. A woman engages in a critical evaluation of her body as part of her preparation for her day. Negative body image is part of a culture that she has been forced to live in. She becomes fluent in the language of derogatory commentary about her physical self; this is a language easily understood by most women. A woman may experience positive thoughts and statements regarding her body in the way she would with an unfamiliar, foreign language. This creative process guides participants to a place of positive self-evaluation, where they are encouraged to practice the metaphoric language of the land. The language is rich with positive descriptive terms related to the many parts of the body that form the whole woman.

Objectives

- Group discussion to explore vulnerability associated with discussion of specific body parts.
- Review of skills to manage emotions learned and practiced in previous experientials.
- Members develop positive affirmations to carry with them through the process.

- Relaxation and guided imagery process to promote a sense of internal calm, while experiencing the body with the mind of a creator and the eyes of an artist.

- Identify positive aspects of specific body parts, to open the door for ongoing, positive self-evaluation. This process introduces a new language that counters the negative messages often seen in mainstream culture—messages that promote unrealistic and potentially unhealthy body types.

- Interactive group process to promote comfort with the language of body *appreciation*. Women practice making positive statements about their own body in the presence of other women.

- Use of a chalk pastel to create a free-flowing outline of the body (not a precise outline), to which are added body parts created from a variety of art materials. Collage is encouraged.

- Incorporate the universal language of music to create a lighter mood, and reduce sense of vulnerability in the process.

- Dialogue and reflection process to practice the language of self-appreciation.

Settings

GROUP DISCUSSION

Arrange chairs in a circle if possible. If that is not possible, try to arrange the chairs so that group members can see each other.

RELAXATION AND GUIDED IMAGERY

Provide space so that participants are able to sit in a chair or lie on the floor (with mats or towels) while engaging in the relaxation and guided imagery process. Offer a low light, or adjusted light if possible. Place a "Do not disturb" sign on the door if you think you could be interrupted. Ask members to turn off their cell phones and other electronic devices before starting the process. Some type of music player is required if you would like to incorporate music into the process.

ART PROCESS

Participants will need adequate table space to develop their images. They will also need a large (approximately 7' (2m) high) piece of white butcher (poster) paper attached to the wall, and a space in front of the paper to work. Chairs should be available for those working at the table and/or the wall. A separate table for art materials is desirable. I also set up a separate work station for the warm glue guns.

- Music: The use of music, as always, is optional. I often use soft, instrumental background music with the relaxation and guided imagery process, as well as the art process. I have also used music that goes with creative work on each body part.

  Examples:

  ○ eyes: "I Only Have Eyes for You" (The Flamingos), "Doctor My Eyes" (Jackson Browne)

  ○ ears: "I Heard it Through the Grapevine" (Marvin Gaye), "Penny Lane" (The Beatles)

  ○ mouth: "Careless Whisper" (George Michael), "Our Lips are Sealed" (The Go-Go's)

  ○ nose: "Nose to the Grindstone" (Artie White)

  ○ stomach: "Yummy, Yummy, Yummy, I've Got Love in My Tummy" (Arthur Resnick, Joey Levine)

  ○ hips: "Twist and Shout" (The Beatles), "Hips Don't Lie" (Shakira)

  ○ feet: "Footloose" (Kenny Loggins), "Knocks Me off My Feet" (Stevie Wonder)

  ○ legs: "Walk on By" (Dionne Warwick), "Legs" (ZZ Top)

  ○ overall: "Your Body is a Wonderland" (John Mayer), "Beautiful" (Christina Aguilera).

- Art materials: Large pieces (approximately 7' (2m) high) of white butcher (poster) paper to hang on the wall. Provide enough pencils, colored pencils, markers, oil pastels and chalk pastels for participants to choose from, should they decide to do a general outline of the body before adding specific parts. (This is not part of the directive, but I have found that some women prefer to create an outline first.) Art materials may also include (but are not limited to): paints, markers, paint pens, colored and decorative paper, glitter or glitter glue, ribbons and strings, magazines, art books, old calendars, tissue and cloth.

Group Discussion

Provide a general introduction to the relaxation and guided imagery process as well as the art experiential. Explore the potential for feelings of vulnerability during the process (because you are working with actual parts of the body), and validate those feelings. Remind participants of the skills they have learned that will help them manage any feelings they may have during this process. Initiate a discussion of those skills/techniques:

- Ability to come back to the moment by grounding the self in a multi-sensory awareness of current experience. (Reduces fear and anxiety associated with the past and the future.)

- Awareness that emotions vary in intensity—they diminish as they are acknowledged and allowed to *move through* the mind and body.

- The purses (developed in the Chapter 6 experiential) carry belongings that help women on their journey.

- Shoes will carry women travelers through their journey and reduce the risk of becoming stuck.

- The heroine within gives each woman strength to face whatever lies ahead.

Discuss possible affirmations that women can develop, write down and repeat to themselves as they move through the process: "I look at myself and feel strength. I feel my breath moving my thoughts and feelings out of my body, into the universe."

Relaxation and Guided Imagery Process

[Speak at a slow pace and allow for frequent pauses.]

Sitting on a chair, or on the floor, find a position that feels comfortable. Close your eyes if you are able to do so. If not, focus your eyes on an area or object in the room—your eyes should feel relaxed. Feel yourself present in the room, in your chair (or on the floor), in this moment of time.

Begin to notice your breath as it moves in and out of your body. Become aware of your breathing. [pause] Feel yourself becoming relaxed and comfortable. Move your attention to your toes and feet. [pause] Feel the muscles in your feet and toes relax. As you breathe out, the tension is released. Feel them light, and at rest. [pause] Continue to be aware of your breath, moving in and out. [pause] Now focus your attention on your legs and thighs. [pause] Feel the muscles in your legs and thighs becoming relaxed, and light. [pause] Continue to breathe in, and out. As you breathe out, release any tension held in your legs and feet. [pause] Focus your attention on your hips and bottom. [pause] Relax the muscles in that area. Feel your entire lower body relaxing, feeling lighter. [pause] Pay attention to your breath, moving in and out of your body. As your breathe out, you release stress held in your body. Move your attention to your stomach and chest. [pause] Relax the muscles in your stomach… and your chest. Feel your stomach relaxing, feeling at rest. Feel your chest becoming more relaxed with each breath that you take. [pause] As you breathe out, release any tension held in your stomach and chest. [pause] Shift your awareness to your upper and lower back. [pause] Relax all of the muscles up and down your back. Feel your back relaxing. Pay attention to your breathing. Breathe in…and out. Release any tension that you hold in your back. [pause] Move your attention to your shoulders and neck. [pause] Relax the muscles there. Feel your shoulders and chest relaxing, feeling lighter. [pause] As you breathe in and out, you are releasing the tension that you hold in your body. Pay attention to your arms, wrists, hands and fingers. [pause] Relax the muscles in your arms and hands. Feel your arms and hands at rest. [pause] Continue to breathe away any tension that you hold in your body. [pause] Move your attention to your head and face. [pause] Relax all of the muscles there. Feel the muscles in your head and face at rest, relaxed. [pause] Breathe slowly and deeply. As you exhale, feel any remaining tension move away. Your muscles are in a restful, relaxed state.

You are aware of yourself, in the room, on the chair (or floor), in this moment of time. [pause] There is no need to worry about yesterday or tomorrow; this is the moment that matters. You allow thoughts and feelings to flow through your mind and body with ease. You are aware of your body, relaxed and in a state of rest. You acknowledge your body as the vehicle that carries you through this life. You thank your body for allowing you to experience the world completely, with all of your senses. You are aware of the many parts of your body that join together to form a whole person. You are that person, deserving of compassion, love and respect. On this day, in this moment, you experience your body with the mind of a creator, and the eyes of an artist.

When you are ready, open your eyes and be present in the room.

You may move to the table to begin the art process.

Art Process
The art process is made up of discussions and directives.

Discussion 1
Participants sit at their workspace and begin with a discussion of body parts that are associated with the face and head. Invite women to explore roles that these body parts play: How are they helpful? What do they do to help achieve goals? The facilitator may have to initiate the process by giving examples:

- eyes:
  - May be the first line of connection to the world.
  - Gatekeepers of our tears.
- nose:
  - Initiates nostalgic thoughts and memories. Smells can take us back in time to our early childhood, or remind us of persons or things that we have known.
  - Holds our glasses and sunglasses on our faces.
- lips/mouth:
  - Entrance to the body for nourishment.
  - Help to form our words in communication.
- ears:
  - Allow us to take in sounds that help us to feel connected to the world.
  - Hold our earrings on our head.

Art Directive 1

> Using drawing, painting or collage materials, create a life-size representation of your face and head [only the face and head at this point]. You may work directly on the large paper [attached to the wall], or develop the image to glue onto the paper.

Discussion 2

Participants return to their workspace for group discussion of body parts associated with the neck and torso. Again, the focus will be on the positive aspects of these body parts.

Examples:

- neck:
    - Carries the head.
    - Pulse; measure of life found there.
- breast:
    - Contains the heart of the woman.
    - Comfort spot for a sad child.
- stomach:
    - Contains and processes food so we can live.
    - Wellspring of emotions.

Art Directive 2

> Again, using any materials available, create a life-size representation of your neck and torso. You can work directly on the large paper [attached to the wall], or develop the image to glue onto the paper.

Discussion 3

Participants return to their workspace for group discussion of hips, thighs and buttocks.

Examples:

- hips:
    - Provide power in sports (i.e. golf swings, batting).

       ◦ Express rhythm and emotion when dancing.

- thighs:

       ◦ Power part of the leg.

       ◦ Help to hold our body upright.

- buttocks:

       ◦ Formed by muscles that move and stabilize the hip joint.

       ◦ Give us something to sit on.

Art Directive 3

> Using any art materials available, create a life-size representation of your hips, thighs and buttocks.

Discussion 4

Participants return to their workspace for group discussion of lower calves and knees.

    Examples:

- calves:

       ◦ Absorb impact from running, jumping, dancing.

       ◦ Hold our socks up.

- knees:

       ◦ Join the thigh and leg.

       ◦ Quiver to show emotion.

Art Directive 4

> Create a life-size representation of your calves and knees. Work on large paper, or attach an image to the paper.

Discussion 5

Participants return to their workspace for group discussion of feet and toes.

Examples:

- feet:

    ○ Allow us to see new places; source of mobility.

    ○ Calm us when they are soaked or massaged.

- toes:

    ○ Help us to maintain our balance.

Art Directive 5

Using any art materials available, create a life-size representation of your feet and toes. Add it to the image you are developing.

Add any other body parts that you would like to include.

Dialogue and Reflection Process

Possible discussion topics:

- Describe how you are feeling in this moment.

- Discuss any vulnerabilities you felt in the process. How did you respond to those feelings?

- As you were moving through the process, how were you experiencing your body (your actual body)?

- Looking at the image that you created, what is it like to see the parts of your self come together to form a whole image of you?

- What was it like to develop an image of your physical body with the mind of a creator, and the eyes of an artist?

Homework

Hang the image you created today on a wall where it is visible to you. Remember to look at yourself (your image) with the eyes of an artist. Continue to think about positive qualities associated with parts of your body. Use colorful pencils or markers to add positive statements to your artwork. Feel free to collage!

Reframe Your Frame

Artist's Statement

For me, I thought about all of the things that a woman's body is capable of. As I did this process, so many emotions came up and I noticed where they were in my body when I glued the images on the paper. I appreciate my body a lot more. I felt how strong a mother's love is and how important her body is in taking care of her kids. I felt sad that I have put my body through so much.

Figure 9.1 Mother tree

Figure 9.2 Ships and moons

10

Tree of Life

Exploration of Self in Nature

INTRODUCTION

Journeys through life are a blend of movement within the physical world around us and dynamic, internal voyages along the vast landscape of our minds, hearts and souls. External journeys typically involve contact with people, places, objects and other living things. During travels within, we meet and interact with the cognitive, emotional, physical and spiritual aspects of self. Actual life journeys of women often differ greatly from romantic and adventure-filled journeys depicted in movies and books. In daily life external journeys commonly include repetitive attention to details, hard work and dedication to people and causes. Women may find joy and contentment in some of their roles, but they are also likely to experience exhausting and repetitive routines in their roles as mothers, daughters, spouses, sisters and colleagues.

While traveling on the journey of life, a woman is likely to encounter cultural and environmental variables in her path. Life scenery often lacks novelty or diversity; the road itself may be rough, blocked or suddenly changing in direction. Unease or fear may occur while walking beneath a storm, or anticipating one off in the distance. Travel weariness may be intensified by the weight of luggage packed with worry about work, family, relationships, finances and other stressors.

A woman traveler may also feel weighed down by self-doubt and negative self-reflections. Women are often inundated with cultural and environmental stimuli that are likely to generate negative thoughts regarding her body, the vehicle that she is traveling in. She may doubt her ability to access resources or master skills that will help her along the way. She may question her worthiness to receive friendship, love or support; this may contribute to her hesitation to reach out to others for help. The day-to-day challenges faced by a woman on her life journey can result in physical, emotional and spiritual fatigue.

Although a woman may value her work and the people she encounters on her journey, she is likely to desire and seek out relief from the emotional and physical toll that environmental stress, obligations and interactions with other travelers may bring. She may find fleeting moments, or hours, to transcend her current life experience by traveling vicariously through the lives of other people and characters presented in novels, movies, games and social network sites. The female market for romance novels, "chick-flicks," computer games, game systems and numerous social networking sites reflects this trend for women to escape the present moment, to experience the life journey through others.

The activities described above often take place in indoor environments such as work or home. Accessibility and affordability of technology have allowed women to bring equipment into their immediate surroundings, where they can be readily and easily accessed. Women read, play games and look at pictures related to life outdoors; however, these experiences are virtual, and lack multi-sensory contact with the world of nature. The advantages of virtual connection to real or imagined places may be contributing to loss of our connection to nature. We have lost our awareness of evolving through nature. We have lost touch with Mother Earth. This lack of vision comes with significant risks.

When a woman is reading about the moon and stars in a romance novel, she is not standing beneath the sky experiencing the full mystery of her innate connection to a world she does not completely understand. When she is watching the story of an adventure on the high seas, she does not feel her feet sinking gently into the sands of the ocean as she ponders her sense of belonging with the great body of water. When playing a computer game that depicts life on farms, she is not stroking the coarse hair on the back of an animal that she somehow feels emotionally connected to. When looking at the smiling faces of her friends on Facebook, she is not stooping down to look into the eyes of a child, sensing that those eyes capture the entire universe in one moment. There is much to be lost.

Women can create a balance on their life journeys by enjoying what technology has to offer while simultaneously seeking out, and practicing, a *grounding* with nature. Women are, and always have been, an integral part of the natural world. It is around us, within us, and the essence of who we are. Not so long ago we lived as part of nature. Technological advancements create an exaggerated sense of time and distance between our past, when we lived outdoors on the land, and the present day, when many dwell mostly indoors. We have a tendency to feel further removed from our original connection to nature than we are. Where do we find nature?

Nature exists in obvious places such as national parks and wildlife reserves. Nature also exists where we do not expect to find it. It occurs in places that are not visible to the human eye without microscope or telescope. It is in the far reaches of the universe, and inside our cells. It prevails in places where we think it could not—in the darkest corners of an abandoned cave, or in the very heart of a bustling city. Nature reveals itself in the green sprout that pushes its way up through the concrete sidewalk, as well as in the magnificence of the sea, or the grace of the mountains.

For many women, true experiences in nature are perceived as rare occurrences that involve investments of time and money—but physical journeys that we take to connect to the world of living things do not have to involve modes of transportation or significant changes in location. One need only step out and look up into the sky, or down toward the ground, or anywhere in between, to experience the extraordinary web of life. The multi-sensory experience of the world outside our front doors reminds us of the simplicity and complexity of life. The simplest action taken to engage with nature may result in a profound richness of experience. When life travelers are not weary from maneuvers through airports and roadways, they may have greater stores of energy for reflection on the natural world.

In the midst of technological advancements that seem to be moving us along at the speed of light, there is a parallel movement that encourages us to slow down and become fully aware of the moment we are in. The practice of mindfulness, or "the awareness that emerges through paying attention on purpose, in the present moment, and nonjudgmentally to the unfolding of experience moment to moment" (Kabat-Zinn, 2003, p.145) enhances all of our life experiences on our journeys. Taking a mindful walk outdoors helps us to become fully present in the world of nature around us, and within us. Fully alive with all of our senses, our awareness of the mystery of nature is enhanced. We experience marvels of the natural world—plants and other life that would typically be ignored, rejected or taken for granted.

Women have an innate sense of connection to the natural world, and their bond with nature helps them to feel part of something greater than themselves. Development of that sense of connection contributes to physical well-being, emotional balance and heightened spirituality. Our relationship with nature reminds us that we are not alone on our life journey. This awareness helps us to put our lives and our life situations into broader perspective, bringing new meaning to our day-to-day experiences.

Throughout history fine artists, poets, songwriters and novelists have drawn from the qualities of nature to depict the physical and emotional climates of characters and environments. The moon is frequently associated with relationships, love sought after, acquired, forgotten or lost. Mountains offer a different perspective of life; a traveler may nestle safely in a valley, or feel exposed to the elements, standing so close to the sky. Descriptions of the ocean bring emotion, depth, color and movement to any visual or written work. Forests, and trees themselves, reflect the physical, emotional and spiritual aspects of human beings—particularly women.

Trees are as physically diverse as women. We are drawn to, and value the existence of, individual trees of different colors, shapes, sizes and characters. We will take time out of a busy day to stop and look at a tree that appears unique, or stands apart from the others. People may travel to different parts of the country, or even the world, to observe trees that have a particular meaning or representation. Trees serve functions when they provide fruit and shade; however, they are also planted as symbols of beauty. Trees remind us that we are connected to nature in some important way.

Trees are universal symbols that reflect the physical, emotional and spiritual qualities that women strongly identify with. Trees have roots that connect them to the earth and draw up nutrients necessary for health and development. Like a tree, a woman metaphorically draws from her roots to maintain life. Women come into the world rooted to their initial caregivers; those roots continue to grow, extending outward to family and friends. When a woman feels grounded and is receiving nourishment from her roots, she intuitively branches out to the physical and spiritual worlds, seeking purpose and belonging. A woman's ideas, creativity and spirituality spread through the roots, creating a broader connection to the immediate and world communities.

Tree branches that reach out towards the skies and heavens are dependent on the sustenance taken in by the roots. A woman is able to take from the world, and give back to the world. The branches of a tree produce leaves and fruit. They provide shelter and homes for many living things. The tree trunk is the connection between roots and branches. This physical structure of the base has similar qualities to the life-giving female body. The bark, like skin, comes in many textures and colors. The height, shape and weight of trees vary tremendously; we value the significance of diversity that they bring to our lives.

Trees serve as valuable projective objects for women. Trees mirror back qualities of self that we are not able to see through eyes that have been conditioned to critique and are blind to the value of what is observable in our physical bodies. Trees teach us about our own roots and initiate reflection about what must be taken in biologically for survival of the body, as well as what is added for the ultimate life and growth of the system as a whole. Trees show us how to reach out to others in our immediate community, to the broader world, and the universe. They show us that we can value and appreciate the uniqueness of our physical, cognitive, emotional and spiritual selves.

Trees are all around us. They are one of the most recognizable aspects of nature, and they serve as constant, accessible teachers, helping us to reconnect to the world of nature and the natural elements that exist within ourselves.

Women are continuing to evolve in nature; therefore we must continue to expand our intrinsic connection to the natural world. As women engage in a mindful exploration of nature, and trees in particular, they will find that the benefits far outweigh the risks of wasting time or failing in the process. As we become consciously aware of the essence of nature and self, we feel alive and genuine. Nature helps us to feel real.

EXPERIENTIAL

Theme

We live in times of great ecological uncertainty. The core relationship we have with Mother Earth comes into question as we explore our sense of connection to the natural world. We look at our impact on a system that seems so powerful, yet so fragile at the same time. The earth's natural environment that sustains us with air, food, warmth and water can be damaged or placed in a state of imbalance, as a result of natural disasters and man-made environmental catastrophes. As humans we seek ways to repair our relationship with the earth and heal injuries to our planet. Nature discloses problems within its own system in the language of depletion, disease and destruction.

A woman may damage her own natural system attempting to maintain or create a body based on unrealistic cultural standards. As women return to an innate connection to nature, balance is restored and there is movement towards the healing of body, mind and spirit.

Metaphors

Women are introduced to the natural world at a very early age through books and the oral tradition of storytelling. Fabulous fairytales and fables include descriptions of magical creatures, faraway lands, plants and animals as well as other imaginary aspects of nature. The natural world depicted in stories includes important symbols that may be stored in the unconscious mind and accessed throughout life. The tree is a particularly meaningful and relevant symbol to many women. As women are guided into the world of nature, they instinctively return to the world of imagination, where the familiar symbol of the tree comes to life as a representation of self.

Objectives

This two-part process incorporates relaxation and creativity by taking a mindful walk into nature to explore a tree with qualities that invite a sense of personal identification with it. In the first part women each identify a tree that seems familiar and easy to relate to. They increase their awareness and appreciation of the physical, emotional and spiritual attributes of self in the second part, by considering aspects of their chosen tree. A non-judgemental awareness is encouraged throughout the process.

Settings

ART PROCESS 1: WALK INTO NATURE

The outdoor setting should have a variety of trees to choose from. This could be a park, a campus or perhaps a block within a chosen neighborhood. The area should allow safety and privacy for participants to stand or sit close to their tree. Group discussion of the mindful walking and sketching process may take place either indoors or outdoors. Privacy should be considered.

Note: If a space to walk in is not available, you can place books that contain images of trees out on a table. Participants can also look at the trees on internet sites if available.

- Music: Participants may bring electronic devices with music if desired.

- Art materials: A sketchpad that can be easily carried. A pencil or other drawing materials. Participants may like to bring a camera to take pictures of their tree. However, this is not required for the art process.

ART PROCESS 2: EXPLORING THE TREE-SELF

Participants will need workspace to develop their trees using a variety of materials. Wall space should be available for participants to hang large (life-size) pieces of paper. Some participants may choose to work on the ground, if space permits.

- Music: Music can be included as desired.

- Art materials: You will need large, life-size pieces of butcher (poster) paper. Precut papers and have them hanging on the wall ahead of time if possible—this can be a time-consuming process. Have a variety of art materials on a large worktable. You should have: markers, colored pencils, paints and brushes. Additional art materials may include (but are not limited to) tissue papers, colored and decorative papers, glitter glue, ribbons, strings, cloth and found objects from nature. If you use heavier materials such as shells, buttons, etc., you should have a glue gun on hand.

Art Process 1: Walk into Nature

Select a location to take a walk. Carry a sketchpad and drawing materials.

If time allows, read the following out loud before beginning the walk. You may provide a copy of the mindful walking exercise (described below) for women to carry with them on the walk.

> Begin to walk slowly into nature. Become aware of your breathing.
>
> As you walk, pay attention to how your body feels in motion. How do your feet feel as they move along the ground? How do they feel when you stop? Are your arms and hands swinging alongside your body, or are they positioned in another way? Does your body feel cold, hot or somewhere in between? What do you see around you? Be sure to look up, down and around. Notice not only the shapes and colors of things that you see, but also how light impacts their appearance. What do you smell? Are the smells subtle or strong? What do you hear? Are the sounds soft or loud? Are they steady, or do they pass? Do the sounds seem close to you, or are they far away? Is there anything in your environment that you could taste? How would you describe the taste?
>
> Take some time for a walk before you begin to select a tree.
>
> If you find your mind drifting off to other thoughts, gently pull yourself back to the moment you are in. Pay attention to your experience of the world through your senses.
>
> Keeping your mind open, with *non-judgemental awareness*, begin to notice the trees around you. Allow your attention to move to any tree or trees that seem to stand out. Is there a tree that seems familiar or comfortable in some way? Does the tree hold your interest? Do you identify with the tree at all? If so, you may have discovered the tree whose image you will develop today.
>
> Remember to breathe, and stay in your multi-sensory experience of your surroundings.
>
> Your tree may be in visual range, but not easily accessible. In this case, you may stand or sit in a place where you can observe your tree.

Read the following out loud before the process, or during the process if possible.

> As you walk around the tree you selected:
>
> - Look at the upper, middle and lower sections of the tree.
> - Place your fingertips on the tree.
> - Trace the outline of parts of the tree with your fingertips.
> - Stand back from the tree. Stand close to the tree. If possible, look at the tree from different perspectives.
> - When you feel ready, begin the art directive.

Art Directive 1

> [You may like to print out the guidance below ahead of time. You may also like to add your own specific considerations.]
>
> Using your paper and pencil, begin a rough sketch of your tree. Consider the physical qualities of the tree, such as:
>
> - possible age of tree
> - texture of wood
> - dampness or dryness
> - color of bark
> - presence of leaves, blossoms or fruit on the branches
> - length of branches
> - location and extension of branches
> - tree's posture
> - wear from age, weather, disease, fire, etc.
>
> Consider the particular psychological aspects of the tree. Does the tree stand alone, or is it in a group of trees? Are the branches reaching out to the world, or the sky, or do they seem more contained to the tree itself? Is the tree providing shade for grass, flowers or shrubs? Is the tree a home for other living things? Does the tree seem to have a mood: is it lifting its branches in celebration or is it drooping as if reflective, tired or in mourning? Does the tree seem to reflect a particular developmental period: is it a curious toddler, a precocious teenager or a wise, elderly woman?

> Take as much time as possible to get to know your tree. Add details to your sketch and jot down any thoughts that come to mind related to your chosen tree.

Dialogue and Reflection Process 1

You may like to print the questions out ahead of time and have them available for participants.

Possible questions for discussion:

- What was it like to walk and relax simultaneously?

- How did you feel while searching for a tree that you could identify with?

- Were you able to take a non-judgemental approach in this process?

- What initially captured your interest in the tree you chose?

- Discuss the qualities (physical, emotional, spiritual) of the tree you selected. Share your sketch if you are comfortable doing so.

- Is there anything you wish you could change about your tree?

- Are there qualities you particularly appreciate about your tree? Do you have any of those qualities? Can you imagine developing these qualities?

- How does the body of the tree relate to your own body?

- Describe anything you became aware of about yourself in your exploration of the tree.

Return the participants to the work area for the next art process.

Art Process 2: Exploring the Tree-Self

This art process encourages a closer exploration of the tree as a projective representation of self. The use of multi-media allows for the maximum development of the tree image and, thus, development of self. The use of a variety of art materials allows for regression in the process, as well as establishment of a greater sense of control. The tree, by nature, serves as a reminder of development and growth—participants may re-experience the developmental stages of their lives during this process. Diversity of the physical, emotional and spiritual aspects of trees is acknowledged and celebrated.

Art Directive 2

Use life-size paper to develop your tree as a representation of who you are. Try to take a non-judgemental approach as you explore many aspects of yourself: physical, emotional, spiritual, developmental, interpersonal and any others that come to mind. Consider sketches and notes from the "Walk into Nature" process.

Using any art materials you choose, bring your tree to life as a representation of yourself.

Dialogue and Reflection Process 2

You may like to print the questions out ahead of time and have them available for discussion.

Possible questions for discussion:

- What is your initial impression of your artwork?

- Is there anything that seems familiar, comforting?

- Is there anything that surprises you?

- Consider the qualities of your tree that you explored in nature. (Refer to the list on page 155.)

- How does the body of your tree relate to, or interact with, the inner workings of your tree?

- Develop an affirmation, e.g. "I am a strong tree, able to weather storms and other unforeseen forces of nature."

Homework

Hang your artwork on a wall at home if possible. Allow the image of your tree to continue to speak to you. Repeat your affirmation throughout the day, for the next several days.

Develop new affirmations. Take mindful walks outdoors—even brief walks can help you to feel part of the natural world. Remember that a woman's innate connection to the world of nature is a vital aspect of the life journey.

Tree of Life

Artist's Statement

My tree is a magnolia tree. There's something about the instant it starts blooming that really catches my eye. It's so beautiful. That's pretty much the only time this tree is recognized. Sometimes I feel as though I'm a magnolia tree. It's like I only stand out when I've done something amazing.

Figure 10.1 Containing energy

Figure 10.2 Magnolia tree

11

Thinking Outside of the Mirror

A Celebration of the Human Body

INTRODUCTION

Women moving through the journey of self-discovery take time to stop and rest for a while. They get comfortable as they prepare to share thoughts, ideas and feelings regarding the cultural expectations of female beauty. The women who join together on this voyage of self-discovery experience a sense of connection as they share the impact of forced cultural values on their lives. Each traveler's perception of self has been affected by the unrealistic, stereotypical images of women that densely cover the landscapes along the roads of life. There appears to be no escape from the concept of the *ideal* female body, because that iconic image has been normalized and integrated into the American mind. Women of all ages are expected to come as close to achieving the ideal as possible. Our culture makes rare exceptions and gives very few passes. Occasionally, an extraordinary female humanitarian may be spared the collective critique of the nation; although she will likely remain fodder for late-night talk show hosts and "Saturday Night Live" comedians. The ever-present reminder of idealized female beauty has contributed to a conditioning of women so that they automatically look to mirrors as reflectors of self-worth.

Almost every environment that a woman moves through contains a mirror. There are tremendous variations in the styles and sizes of mirrors: hand-held mirrors, wall mirrors, rear-view mirrors, make-up mirrors, bathroom mirrors, dressing-room mirrors and elevator mirrors. These examples represent just a few variations in the vast world of mirrors. Certain types of mirrors used by women in their daily routines do not reflect the entire self. As a woman looks into her make-up mirror, she only sees the part of herself that the dimensions of the mirror allow. She is "framed" within the reflective surface; the mirror becomes a metaphoric container for the physical self. A woman generally accepts the limited, surface-level information that a mirror reflects back to her; much of her identity becomes bound to the ritual of physical evaluation in the mirror. She may become afraid to step away from the reflection to look at other parts of her self. The mirror distracts a woman from exploring the internal qualities of self that she rejects or fears: her perceived character flaws, mistakes she has made in her life, her intense emotional states. As long as she explores herself in the mirror with a critical eye, she is not looking at the parts of herself, or her life, that may bring pain, fear or other seemingly unmanageable feelings. She has found the perfect, culturally sanctioned coping mechanism.

Women form relationships with their mirrors. They are not real-life relationships; however, women often describe their connection to mirrors in terms that would be used for actual relationships: "My mirror is my best friend," or "My mirror is my worst enemy." A woman may become trapped in a type of rapprochement relationship with her mirror. She longs for her own unique identity in the world, yet she has difficulty tolerating extended periods of separation from the object that defines her. Her return to the mirror to check her reflection temporarily reduces her anxiety. The mirror takes on the role of parental approval or disapproval. If the mirror-object reflects back an image of the woman that would meet the cultural standards for beauty, then she is a *good girl*. If the image reflected back from the mirror falls short of those standards, then she sees herself as a *bad girl*.

The multi-billion dollar diet and beauty industries, like the mirror, become extended "false parents" to women seeking love and approval. These industries, driven by phenomenal profits, have created a type of "smoke and mirrors" advertising to cloud women's perception of themselves. Western women are also losing their capacity to see, and address, what is happening in the broader culture. Western societies are experiencing a juxtaposition of the *ideal* and the *real*. In the twenty-first century women face body issues related to physical and mental illness, aging, war and economics. Diseases such as skin cancer, breast cancer, diabetes and autoimmune disorders often lead to changes in physical appearance. Chronic stress, anxiety and depression, which seem to be at epidemic levels, may contribute to changes in the body, such as hair loss and dermatological conditions. We have an aging population of baby boomers; the process of aging affects the appearance of the human body. Women veterans, injured in military service, may experience profound losses and changes upon, and within, their bodies. Economic factors such as job loss, causing inability to pay for dental treatment, have resulted in neglect of teeth. Yet our culture continues to demand an unrealistic, stereotypical standard of beauty.

Corporate advertisements displayed on the waters and roadways of life appeal to a woman's insecurities by showing her what she doesn't possess, but could have. The diet, exercise, beauty and cosmetic surgery industries know what they are doing. They promote weight loss and other physical alterations as a means of finding happiness. Spokeswomen for these programs have big smiles—they seem exceptionally happy. Valerie Bertinelli, Carrie Fisher, Jennifer Hudson and Mariah Carey inspire American women to get thin, so they can be happy too. The *unspoken* message is clear: "I have talent, money, an amazing life, and I will be happy as soon as I am thin." We don't hear the women talk about things that they appreciate and cherish about themselves. We don't hear their gratitude for having a body-vehicle that carries them through this amazing life.

Women who gather together to travel the road of self-discovery begin to counter corporate-driven cultural standards of beauty by utilizing the object that perpetuates the problem: the *mirror*. Working within a safe and validating environment, participants are asked to draw a picture of themselves standing in front of a mirror. The directive is kept very open so that women will bring their own experience to the process. Participants sometimes ask if they should include clothes in the image, and I tell them that they may draw whatever comes to mind. The image of the mirror creates a natural *frame* that contains anxiety experienced in the process. Some women emphasize the borders of the mirror, while others draw light outlines.

Travelers are reminded that they may encounter rough waters or roadways while on their journey, and they are encouraged to utilize their coping strategies. For example, I place a chair off to one side of the room, with a focal point (e.g. a bowl with shells) nearby; women may move to that resting place if anxiety is heightened. They are encouraged to return when they feel ready to do so. I remind participants of the skills they have practiced in the art processes described so far in this book. The women then gather together to talk about their experience of imagining themselves standing in front of a mirror. For many women, this may be the first opportunity to discuss mirrors outside of the usual context. This group discussion initiates a shift in how women conceptualize the experience of the mirror; it is explored as a part of an important issue that affects the well-being of women.

During the second art process, women are asked to tap into their mind's eye to draw an image of themselves as they would be if they lived life feeling *healthy and whole*. The definition of "healthy" and "whole" is explored prior to the process, and throughout the process. The women are directed to begin by imagining that they are looking into the reflection of their own eyes. For some women, this is a profoundly different approach to exploring themselves in the mirror. A woman's habit may be to look immediately for flaws and imperfections. They are encouraged to look for strength, wisdom and compassion in their own eyes. The guide (facilitator) reassures travelers that, although they may witness sad emotions in their reflections, those emotions will not overwhelm them. Women are encouraged to explore the parts of self that are "unacceptable"; they return to the reflection of their own eyes in the mirror if anxiety becomes heightened, or feels unmanageable. Travelers begin to experience their body-vehicle with appreciation and respect.

When a woman focuses only on that which is visible in the mirror, the cognitive, emotional and spiritual aspects of self that are contained within the body are pushed into the shadows. Women reclaim their own definition in the world by bringing all of the qualities of self into the light of conscious awareness, where they are explored and integrated into the concept of self. Her body is appreciated and celebrated as the journey of self-discovery continues.

EXPERIENTIAL

Theme

An important aspect of planning a trip is consideration of the numerous forms of transportation that are available to us. We make decisions regarding how we will get from one place to another based on a variety of factors, including accessibility, scheduling, cost and comfort. We also rely upon our bodies to take us through our journeys in life. We are traveling, always, with our bodies. We may become so focused on how our physical appearance is perceived by others that we lose sight of the importance of caring for the body-vehicle that moves us through our journeys. The art process in this chapter teaches participants that the image of *self* in the mirror is not to be avoided. The image of *body* as reflected back from a mirror can actually expand the awareness and appreciation of the physical, emotional and spiritual qualities of *self*.

Metaphors

The mirror is developed as an object that reflects back qualities of the self. A woman's view of her physical body, as seen in an imagined mirror, is explored beyond limited cultural perspectives.

Objectives

- Reflection process to explore communication between mind and body to promote appreciation of this interactive process. Facilitator reads an affirmation that reinforces the communication between mind and body.

- Art process to explore how we see ourselves reflected in the mirror, as well as how we would see ourselves if we lived a life focused on health and wholeness.

- Stream-of-consciousness writing to explore meaning in the artwork.

- A definition of health and wholeness is offered in the reflection process.

Settings

REFLECTION

Provide a space where participants can sit comfortably during the reflection process.

ART PROCESS

Provide adequate table or surface space for drawing or collage work. A separate table may be provided for art materials.

DIALOGUE AND REFLECTION

Provide a quiet space where participants can sit or lie down comfortably while engaging in the dialogue and reflection process. Chairs or mats should be placed in a circle formation, if possible.

- Music: A music player is required to play music during the process if desired.

- Art materials: Art materials include: paper large enough for two images of reflection in mirrors; glue; scissors; pencils; magazines and pictures.

Reflection Process

Take a moment to consider how your body and mind communicate with each other. When you are tired, or hungry or thirsty, your body tries to communicate those needs by sending out signals. These signals may be experienced in ways such as small pangs of discomfort in your stomach when you begin to feel hungry; a dry sensation in your throat when thirst arrives; yawning or stretching when fatigue starts to set in. Sometimes these signals are responded to by the mind, and sometimes they are ignored. The body, in its determination to be heard, will send stronger signals, or create new ones.

There are times when the mind will try to move the body into compliance with its needs. For example, on a day when you think about sitting down to read a good book, your body shifts into position to accommodate that activity. The communication goes both ways. Your body sends signals to your mind that require an intellectual response—for instance, you may become aware of discomfort in a particular part of your body and turn to online research to explore possible explanations for the pain. Many of us have experienced trips to the doctor's office where we find that our pain and discomfort have ceased as we sit in the waiting room. Perhaps the signals are no longer needed because we have already responded.

Your body and mind are also in steady interaction as emotions are experienced. There are times when the body seems to signal to the mind that a feeling is being experienced. Sensations such as butterflies in the stomach, or feeling wound up like a top, may be physical indicators of feelings that precede conscious awareness of the feeling. Then there are times when the feeling seems to be experienced in the mind, in conscious awareness, and then moves to the body. If you receive happy news, you may be consciously aware of your joy before it manifests in your body.

Our spiritual needs are also communicated back and forth between mind and body. There are times when we seek a spiritual state of mind and direct our body into a way of being that complements our desire. For example, the mind may direct the body to move into positions such as sitting or kneeling for prayer or meditation. Then there are times when the body seems to be directive when seeking a spiritual way of being. For example, you may suddenly become aware of anxious movements of your body and respond by stepping out into nature for a mindful walk.

On our life journey we may become so busy or distracted that the lines of communication between mind and body are weakened. The mind, in a heightened emotional state or in defensive mode, may disregard the signals that the body sends. We are able to open the doors of communication so that the mind and body are able to guide each other in working towards optimal wellness of the system.

Affirmation

> Your body and mind are in communication with each other. You are tuned into your body's physical cues, responding to them with wisdom and compassion. You are able to integrate all aspects of well-being, considering physical, intellectual, emotional and spiritual needs.

Art Process 1

Women imagine themselves standing in front of a mirror, and on one half of their sheets of paper, they draw the image that they see. They write about the image, and then share their thoughts in a group process.

Art Directive 1

Tap into your mind's eye to find an image of how you see yourself in a full-length mirror. Using one half of your sheet of paper, draw the image that you see.

Take approximately five minutes to write about your image.

Dialogue and Reflection Process 1

Possible questions for discussion:

- What was it like to imagine/draw/develop your image?

- What is your overall impression of your image/drawing/ picture?

- Was your focus on areas of your body that you appreciate, or was your focus on areas of your body that you are least comfortable with?

- What is the mood, or emotional state, of the person depicted?

- What were your feelings during this process? Did they change as you looked at different areas of your body?

- Describe yourself as the observer—the person who shows up in your shoes to travel the road of self-reflection.

- Is there anything you would like to add to the image, or take away from the image?

Art Process 2

Women then create a second image of themselves standing in front of a mirror, which they draw alongside the first one: this image reflects a focus on *health and wholeness*. They also write about this image and share thoughts and feelings in a group process. The body-vehicle is appreciated for all that it does to take the female traveler on her journey through life.

Art Directive 2

[Speak at a slow pace and allow frequent pauses.]

Tap into your mind's eye to find an image of how you would see yourself in a full-length mirror if you lived a life feeling healthy and whole. You will draw this image alongside the first one.

Begin by looking into the reflection of your eyes. [pause] You are not looking around your eyes, but *into* your eyes. [longer pause] You are looking at the wisdom that you have accumulated over the years. [pause] You are looking at the strength that you know you have, because you have worked through problems and have overcome obstacles in your life. [pause] You see the compassion that you feel for others, and can learn to feel for yourself. [longer pause] You see your own sorrow, but it does not overwhelm you. [pause] You see hints of playfulness and a sense of humor. [pause] Explore the image reflected back from the mirror with a childlike curiosity; with a desire to explore without judgement or expectations of how you should look. [longer pause] Allow your gaze to move to other parts of your body. First, notice parts of yourself that you don't often look at. If you find an area of your body that seems unacceptable, [pause] move your gaze back to your eyes and look for wisdom, strength, compassion and humor. [longer pause] Carry these attributes with you as you continue your journey of self-discovery, reflected in the mirror. Be aware of the possibilities of how different parts of your body communicate, and work together. Now consider your body as a vehicle that has transported you on your life journey. [pause] Every single part of your body-vehicle has helped to make your journey possible; none are insignificant. [pause] Take a moment to appreciate the contribution of each part of your body. [longer pause]

Take approximately five minutes to write about this image.

Dialogue and Reflection Process 2

Possible questions for discussion:

- What was it like to imagine/draw/develop your image?

- What were some qualities of yourself that were not apparent in the reflection of your body, but which you became aware of during the process?

- What was the level of difficulty or ease, compared to the first image?

- Looking at your drawing, have you represented physical, intellectual, emotional and spiritual health and wholeness? If so, please describe.

- Were you able to come up with possibilities for how parts of the body communicate with each other?

- If not, do you have a sense of what held you back? Can you identify areas that were more difficult than others?

- What is the mood or emotional state of the person depicted?

- Is there anything that you could place around the figure (i.e. symbol of strength, warmth, creativity, determination, etc.) to feel a stronger sense of health and wholeness?

Drawing variations to consider:

- A drawing of a woman who represents the cultural stereotype of beauty.

- A drawing of a woman your age.

- An image of a woman cut from a magazine or picture. (This variation may reduce anxiety for participants who have resistance to drawing.)

Homework

Practice looking at yourself in the mirror, first making eye contact with yourself, and then seeking qualities of self that reflect health and wholeness. For example, explore the ability of the eyes to express wisdom, knowledge and/or compassion. Do your eyes reflect a rested state of your body, or are they telling you that you need more sleep? How does the growth and condition of your skin, hair and nails reflect the health of your body? What messages are those parts of your body sending to you so that you can continue on a healthy path, or make positive changes? Explore other parts of your body and consider their ability to communicate with each other.

Develop an affirmation—for example: "I view my body with respect and compassion. I appreciate my body's ability to transport me through life. I listen to the needs of my body."

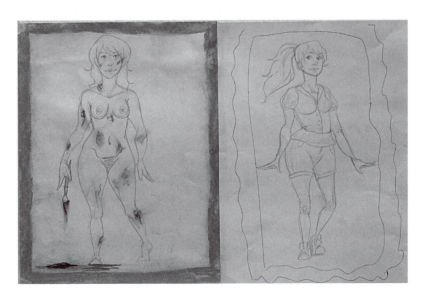

Figure 11.1 Splashes of color/my favourite outfit

Thinking Outside of the Mirror

Artist's Statement

I am looking at myself in an oval mirror because I like oval mirrors and I see myself as "oval" when I'm nude. I'm well proportioned and beige. I didn't include my face because, when looking at myself naked, the expression on my face is of no interest or concern to me.

In the next image, I have a huge brain and it's busy. I have hands to hold. My breasts are large and saggy from nursing babies. My pubic area gives me pleasure. My legs are strong and my feet keep me standing. I see my eyes now.

Figure 11.2 My oval self/alive

Figure 11.3 Hard to see/I see me

12

A Vase of Flowers

Depicting Self in Still Life

INTRODUCTION

As women travel through their journeys in life, they experience many people, places and objects along the way. Some encounters occur by chance, and some have been planned in the itinerary. Women are naturally drawn to surroundings that they feel positive associations with. They form relationships with people that they meet, and they also form relationships with objects that they somehow feel connected to. Marketing strategists, who understand women and object relations, place countless advertising billboards along the road of life. These ads are designed to convince women that they must have particular products (objects) to assist them in meeting the cultural expectation of beauty. Women are taught that they must *look* worthy, in order to be worthy, of love. Of course, as long as there are new products to be sold, and novel services to be rendered, they will not be permitted to feel deserving of love.

A woman's natural tendency to connect with objects that help her feel valuable and worthy of love can be tapped and used to her advantage. There are some objects that women relate to easily; in the creative process these objects become mirrors that reflect back the internal and external qualities of self. Many women feel an association with *flowers*, which are found in abundance along the road of life. By the time a woman has reached the end of the road, she has likely come across a myriad of flowers, diverse in physical nature and symbolic meaning. An object that is closely associated with flowers is the *vase*. The still-life form of a vase holding flowers is a familiar object that has substantial projective qualities for women.

Before a baby girl makes her entrance into the world, she has been exposed to flowers by means of her mother's contact with them.

Mothers-to-be have been known to plant flowers in the garden, or pick flowers to place around the house, honoring an instinctual connection to nature during pregnancy. Pictures depicting images of flowers may be scattered throughout the house: flowers growing wild in fields and meadows, and flowers growing in containers that are as diverse as the flowers themselves; colorful and artsy flowers may dance across the fabric of the mother's maternity outfit. The flowers are reminders of the new life within. Just as flowers draw life-sustaining nutrients through the stem, the baby receives what is needed for life through the umbilical cord. Although the unborn child is blissfully unaware of the flowers in her environment, she is affected by her mother's mood in response to flowers. Once the child enters the world, she may sense her mother's emotions as she receives (or does not receive) flowers in her hospital room. This is a crucial time for the mother to feel connected to those she loves; flowers are messengers that express feelings of love and caring from others.

The cultural association between baby girls and flowers is apparent in the designs of her infant clothing and accessories. She may go home from the hospital wrapped in a floral design blanket, with a large daisy attached to her headband. As her eyes become able to focus, she may concentrate on dangling flowers that hang from a contraption over her head. As soft music from the wind-up box accompanies the dance of the flowers on the mobile, she learns to associate flowers with comfort. As she peers beyond the bars of her crib, she may see images of flowers on wallpaper, blankets, curtains and rugs. Her first pyjamas, shirts, pants and dresses will include flower designs: colorful daisies, tulips and sunflowers splashing across the soft material. As she gets older, she will have backpacks, umbrellas, boots and hats with sprinkles of flowers on the materials. The cups and plates she uses for her tea parties will most certainly have floral patterns; she will learn the importance of placing a vase with a flower in it on the center of the table to brighten the atmosphere of the party.

When she enters preschool, she will continue to experience flowers in books that she is introduced to. She will learn about faraway lands with flowers that grow in the fields, forests, ponds and mountainsides. She will express curiosity about fanciful worlds like the one with magical poppies that cause travelers to fall asleep; or the planet inhabited by a vain, talking rose and a prince who travels to foreign lands. She will bring flowers to life with crayons, markers and paint; they will sparkle with glitter and pretend jewels. She will be introduced to the enchanting world of three-dimensional flowers made of clay, tissue and fabric. When a young girl first holds a paper flower attached to a pipe cleaner, and is able to twirl the flower so she can fully experience the object standing in the world, her identification with the flower is profound. She may move her head or body to mimic the posture of the flower; she may begin to dance while holding the flower in front of her, as if taking cues from it.

As a girl travels the stretch of road we call adolescence, flowers will continue to be an important part of her life. It is likely that flowers will have a significant role in ceremonies such as formal dances, religious celebrations and rites of passage. She may use flowers to help express how she is feeling. A red rose, for example, may reflect one particular mood; white, yellow and pink roses may be used to express other moods. Images of flowers may also reflect cognitive, emotional or physical development. Her interest in simple flowers such as daisies and daffodils may be replaced by a desire for flowers such as roses, orchids and lilies. An adolescent girl understands that there is a broad, exciting world around her; the exotic flower is a representation of her participation in that world. She may look to flowers as confirmation of acceptance by peers. Best friends, potential friends and love interests often share flowers with each other at this age.

As she moves through adolescence, a young woman may begin to fantasize about the flowers she will choose for another important day of her life: her wedding. Flowers truly are the centerpiece of the simplest and most elaborate ceremonies. Flowers used in rituals are selected with much consideration; they are chosen to symbolize what is beautiful and valuable. The flowers that she holds and surrounds herself with on that special day are representations of who she is in the world. She becomes like the flower she has created. Her strength, confidence and certainty of true beauty shine through the day. At the very end of her life, other people will select flowers to depict her presence in the world: a beautiful flower who lived and danced and returned to the earth. The memories of her life, with flowers, go with her.

The earliest memories of flowers, or experiences associated with flowers, become important bookmarks in the photo albums of the mind. Most women are able to recall events or experiences from childhood that involve flowers. I am amazed by the universal ability of women to recall other women who have loved or appreciated flowers in their lives. Many women attending group have revealed stories of grandmothers who gathered bouquets from their own gardens to place on display in the house. Women recall very specific events from childhood; memories of lilac, tulip and daffodil festivals; as well as celebrations that mark seasons of the year, heritage and memorials of special people. One woman in group told the story of an annual planting ceremony beneath the light of the moon with her mother and her sister. Another woman described the happiness she felt each year on the first day of May as she anticipated the basket of flowers that would be left on her porch. Women commonly recall flowers as focal aspects of holidays, anniversaries, graduations and other childhood celebrations.

The vase, a container or holder of the flowers, is also an important object that women identify with. If you walked into the home of any woman, regardless of age, ethnicity or socio-economic status, you would be likely to see some type of vase, or a potential vase. Mason jars, pitchers, water glasses, plastic water bottles and coffee cups all serve as vases in a pinch. When a woman is given a flower, there is an almost instinctive response to place it into a container with water; bouquets of flowers practically cry out to be held by a vase.

Flowers have symbolic meanings that are generally understood by women. For example, the archetypal red rose is collectively recognized as a symbol of love; yellow roses signify friendship; violets represent simplicity; lilies reflect purity. A bouquet that includes a variety of flowers such as roses, lilies, daisies, carnations and other flowers may throw a woman off the trail of interpretation. She may wonder silently or out loud, "What does this mean?" She may call upon her friends, family members or even the internet to help her understand the true meaning of the bouquet. One thing is certain: women have a curiosity regarding the unspoken language of the stemmed messengers. As a woman beholds a flower in front of her, the meaning she finds may be one that is universally recognized, or it may be personal, unique to herself and her situation, or a combination of both.

We may draw upon our inherent interest, familiarity and appreciation of flowers to explore parts of ourselves that lie within. One woman in group referred to the "relationship" we have with flowers as one that can guide us in developing a deeper relationship with ourselves. Flowers are often placed in close vicinity where they are easily seen. They are admired and scrutinized for beauty and imperfections; they are frequently checked for indications that they are coming to the end of their life. During the first moments of contact with cut flowers, a woman registers her awareness that the flowers will soon die. We know that the life of each flower is short: the blooms will fade, wilting will occur, and eventually the ritual of removal must take place. Our acceptance that flowers are with us briefly enforces a mindful presence with them. Each moment has significance.

I have heard some women say that they do not like to have flowers around, because it is sad to see them decline and die off so quickly. They express concern that buying flowers is a waste of money. We may experience a similar resistance when considering aspects of self within. Why waste an emotional investment in something that will very likely bring a sense of loss and pain?

The act of entering into a relationship with an object involves risk. By allowing ourselves to care profoundly, or love deeply, we become vulnerable to potential loss of that which we are attached to. Our relationship with ourselves will not be disappointing if we do not allow it to become profound, or deep. We may defend against possible pain, loss and grief by not becoming significantly attuned and connected to ourselves. Instead, we focus on the outside of who we are—the part that can be altered with diets, plastic surgery and products that slow the effects of time. The vast army of miracle workers in these fields is relentlessly committed to making sure that we feel good about ourselves based solely on how our body appears to the world. We feed this army with self-doubt, fear of rejection and above all with our reluctance to get to know ourselves on a level that could bring the most meaning to our lives.

We can use our innate connection with flowers to enrich the process of cultivating a meaningful relationship with self. Just as we can tolerate the imperfections of flowers, we can learn to tolerate imperfections in ourselves. Imperfect flowers, and weeds, grow together with other flowers in the garden of life. If tended so that they do not overwhelm the garden, the flawed flowers and weeds contribute to an overall natural beauty of the garden. If a traveler walking the road of life ignores gardens and fields out of fear of encountering imperfections, then the journey will surely have less meaning. If we look away from the billboards along the road of life, and are able to explore ourselves beyond cultural definition, we will come to feel worthy of love. Like the vase holding the flowers, we will shine with life and beauty.

EXPERIENTIAL
Theme

As women travel down the road of life, many people, places and things are encountered along the way. Women naturally seek out people and environments that they have positive associations with. Women may also feel drawn to particular objects because of projective identification with the objects. A vase of flowers contains features that many women identify with: physical form, emotional quality and nostalgic content. This workshop begins with a relaxation and guided imagery process that promotes a calm, mindful presence while exploring an imagined vase and flowers. Participants are encouraged to take a non-judgemental approach while creating a vase that depicts the qualities of their own bodies. The flowers that will fill the vase are representations of personal qualities found beneath the skin. The art experiential accompanying the relaxation and guided imagery process promotes a natural projection of the internal and external qualities of self onto the still-life form.

Metaphors

Vases vary significantly in shapes and sizes; they hold flowers which are also diverse in color, form, shape and texture. Vases are "holders" of the flowers. They serve as symbolic representations of a woman's body, the container of all other qualities of self. The flowers may reflect the internal qualities of self, such as compassion, kindness, humor, creativity, intuition, intelligence, courage, determination and spirituality. The flowers may also signify the qualities of self that are disliked, feared and/or rejected. Getting to know ourselves on a deeper level, and learning to appreciate ourselves as whole human beings, requires an exploration of all qualities within. This process of self-reflection is evident in rich and diverse flower arrangements created during the art experiential.

Objectives

- Women explore vases filled with flowers and/or pictures of flowers placed around the room. This process promotes a stronger association with objects that will be developed in the art process.

- Participants engage in a relaxation and guided imagery process to reinforce a mindful presence, while allowing thoughts and feelings to move through mind and body. They prepare to enter the world of the imagination.

- During the relaxation and guided imagery process, each participant imagines a vase as a symbolic representation of her physical body. She imagines flowers that represent personal qualities of self that lie beneath the skin. Women picture themselves placing their flowers inside of the body-vase.

- In the art process, participants bring their vases of flowers to life, and explore all of the qualities of self that have been symbolically depicted.

- Participants practice talking about their bodies, and qualities of self in language that includes positive affirmations. Perceived negative qualities of self are not avoided, but integrated into the overall design of *self as a vase of flowers*.

Settings

Relaxation and Guided Imagery

Provide a quiet space where participants can sit or lie down comfortably while engaging in the relaxation and guided imagery process. Offer adjusted light if possible. Consider placing a "Do not disturb" sign on the door to avoid interruptions. A music player is required to incorporate music into the process. Participants should have paper and a writing tool to jot down notes following this process. If possible, have a few vases with flowers in them at different locations in the room. You may want to use silk flowers to avoid potential allergic responses. Possible examples of vases: mason jars, tall and short glasses, decorative vases, perhaps a dish to float flowers in. The vases and artificial flowers may be purchased at garage sales, thrift stores or even dollar stores (pound shops). I also place images of actual flowers (with their names) on a table or wall in the room.

Art Process

Participants will need adequate table space to develop their still-life forms. Some women may prefer to place their paper on the wall and stand while working. I provide chairs so that participants who work on the wall will have the opportunity to sit down periodically. Provide a separate, long table for art materials. Provide each member with a piece of 11" × 13" (28cm × 33cm) paper in which to develop their image.

- Music: Music that is primarily instrumental in nature helps to create a relaxed setting. I play the music on low volume so that it becomes more of a background sound rather than a primary focus in the process.

- Art materials: Paper in various sizes and colors, pencils, markers, paints and brushes. This process may also incorporate collage (depending on time and availability of materials). Materials for collage: glue, glue gun, glitter glue, colored and decorative papers, beads, ribbons and strings, tissue, cloth and any found objects from nature.

Relaxation and Guided Imagery Process

[Speak at a slow pace and allow frequent pauses.]

Sitting on a chair or on the floor, find a position that feels comfortable while keeping your neck and back as straight as possible. Close your eyes. If you do not feel comfortable closing your eyes, then find a focal point in the room where you can set and relax your eyes. Take a deep, cleansing breath and feel the air moving through your body, down into your abdomen. Feel the warm energy of each breath. [pause] The stress and tension that you carry in your body are moving away as you breathe out. [pause] As you exhale, gently push the air out of your body. [pause] Continue breathing in and out, feeling your body relax. [pause]

As thoughts and feelings come into your mind, allow them to move through, like waves of the ocean or clouds in the sky. Your breathing confirms the life flowing through you, the life within you.

[pause] Relaxed and calm, you are prepared to enter the world of the imagination. Tapping into your mind's eye, picture a vase that represents how you see your body. [pause] Allow a few moments for this image to take shape in your mind. [longer pause] Consider the size and shape of the vase. [pause] Are the sides of the vase linear, parallel or do they curve, moving inward and outward in places? [pause] What is your vase made of? [pause] Is it glass, metal, ceramic or some other material? [pause] Imagine tracing the outline of your vase with your fingertips: [pause] is your vase smooth? [pause] Is it rough or bumpy? [pause] Does your vase feel warm or cool to the touch? [pause] Is your vase solid in color, or can you see through it? [pause] Does the image of the vase change with any shifts in light? [pause] Keep in mind that the image of your vase is developing, based on a representation of your own body.

Remember to pay attention to your breathing throughout this process. Feel the life force moving through you, and within you. [pause] Now consider the qualities of self that lie beneath your skin: compassion, kindness, humor, creativity, intuition, intelligence, courage, determination, spirituality and other characteristics that you identify with. [pause] Allow any judgemental thoughts or feelings to move through you as you also consider the qualities of self that you dislike or reject. Bring them into the forefront of your mind so that they can be looked at and explored. Remember that all of these qualities may be found in the garden of life. When placed into a bouquet, they capture the essence or wholeness of who you are. [pause] Set your vase aside for a few moments. [pause]

Continue to breathe in and out, slowly and deeply, while allowing images of flowers to come forward in your mind. [pause] Imagine the way that each flower represents one quality of self that you considered, or another quality that comes to mind. Perhaps the rose represents the love that you have for your family; or maybe the sunflower symbolizes the strength you bring to your work and hobbies; the dandelion may remind you of a quality such as shyness. Your flowers will have their own meaning for you. Focus for a moment on one flower that comes to mind. [pause] Imagine your hands gently lifting the flower for closer examination. [pause] How does the flower feel as you hold it? [pause] What is the color, or colors, of the flower? [pause] Does the flower change appearance as you move it around in the light? [pause] Does the flower appear as a new bud? Is it a flower in late bloom? [pause] Lift the flower to your nose and breathe in… What do you smell? [pause] Hold the flower up to your lips… What do you taste? [pause] Picture yourself tracing the outline of each flower with your fingertips. Feel the parts of the flower, such as the petals and leaves... Imagine all of these parts coming together to form the whole flower. [pause]

Bring your vase back into the presence of your mind's eye. Picture your hands placing each flower into the vase until you achieve a bouquet that feels complete. Imagine that each flower is able to *speak* to where it belongs in the bouquet. [long pause]

[I encourage participants to imagine that the flowers have a voice, that they become guides in the process. This letting go of having the bouquet appear in just a certain way promotes the participation of the unconscious mind in the process.]

Picture yourself standing back to look at the vase with flowers that you have created. The vase, or the physical body, is holding the internal qualities of self. Together, the vase and flowers form the image as a whole. The vase without the flowers would stand alone as an empty vessel. Without the flowers, the vase may have decorative qualities, but it would not fully accomplish what it was created for. The flowers without the vase would lie flat on the surface and would not be seen or appreciated. Without the water contained in the vase, the flowers would die quickly. The vase and flowers are dependent on each other to reach their full potential. Your body, like the vase, is the holder of qualities within. When your body stands alone, without the shining presence of qualities beneath the skin, it becomes subject to brief, surface-level consideration and admiration. The flowers reflect the diversity and complexity of who you truly are. They bring the mystery of what lies beneath the skin to life. Thus the image of the vase and flowers together truly captures the hearts and minds of the viewer.

Open your eyes now, and when you are ready, become fully present in the room.

Take a few moments to jot down thoughts, feelings and images from the guided imagery process.

Allow approximately a half hour for notes/sketches. I suggest a break before moving into the art process.

Art Process

The relaxation and guided imagery process promotes a sense of identification with an imagined vase of flowers. The process of rendering a vase of flowers in the creative process brings the image to the conscious mind, where it can be fully experienced and incorporated into a self-schema.

> Using any materials you desire, depict yourself as a vase of flowers.

If you do not have a variety of materials, you can direct the group to draw (with colored pencils, markers, etc.) or paint themselves as a vase of flowers.

Dialogue and Reflection Process

Possible questions for discussion:

- Were you able to allow thoughts and feelings related to judgement of yourself to move through, as you engaged in the guided imagery and art process?

- What would you like to say about your picture?

- How does your vase represent your own body?

- Did you face challenges or difficulties as you developed your vase?

- Name the positive qualities of your vase. Relate them to your own body.

- What qualities of self do your flowers represent?

- Were there any qualities that were difficult for you to consider?

- Name the positive qualities of your flowers. Relate them to your own internal qualities.

- What would your vase be without the flowers you created?

- What would your flowers be without the vase you created?

- What did you learn about yourself in this process?

Homework

> Place your picture of your vase of flowers in a visible location. As you continue to practice relaxation and guided imagery, *feel* the part of yourself that is the body, or the holder, of the flowers. Remember the qualities of self that transformed into the flowers

you created. Imagine where each of those qualities may be found within your body. The practice of exploring parts of self that come together to form your vase of flowers is ongoing. Continue to add flowers as you become aware of the different qualities of self.

A Vase of Flowers

Artist's Statement

I started to draw the vase first and then noticed that the shape kind of looked like my own body. I could see my curves and it felt OK. I knew I was going to add color—and the color seemed to add beauty to the vase. I thought about the different parts of myself and imagined what each part would look like as a flower. I like the variety of the bouquet. This was a very different way of looking at my body. I want to put the picture up and look at it longer. That is different than the mirror for me.

Figure 12.1 Sparkles and water

Figure 12.2 Container for a relationship

13

Heads and Tales

Creating a Body for Life

INTRODUCTION

Every woman in our broad and diverse world community walks through her own personal journey in life. There may be subtle or glaring differences among travelers; however, by virtue of being alive, every woman is on a voyage. The journey itself contains story lines: self-authored tales of events and interactions, of relationships encountered along the way. These stories contain significant personal and environmental variables, some observable and others less obvious. Geographical location; political climate; socio-economic standing; religion; spirituality; roles and treatment of women within a culture; intellectual, creative and athletic abilities; genetic predispositions; exposure to trauma; resiliency; health status; motivation; and perception of self—these are just a few factors that create differences... and contribute to unique experiences within each journey. There is, however, one commonality shared by all women: each life traveler receives just one physical body for the life journey. Our bodies are the *vehicles* that move us through real-life adventure tales. As we author the tales of our lives, we are able to identify, develop and appreciate our *body for life*.

There are times when a woman travels down a road that appears linear, with no bends or turns in sight. Some roads are curvy and lack certainty of direction on the horizon. Unlike an actual real-life journey, it is possible for a woman to walk two or more roads on her metaphoric life voyage. Women often do walk parallel roads related to body image: while walking down the road of body appreciation, a woman focuses on developing or maintaining a physical form that is likely to be perceived favorably by the culture; at the same time she may walk the road of body devaluation, engaging in rejection, concealment or alteration of the parts of self that she considers unacceptable, or below cultural standards. When this occurs the result is often a distorted over-evaluation of the external body, and loss of the self that exists beneath the skin. Opportunities to optimize the sense of *wholeness* may be lost. The journey to explore that which lies beneath the skin is rich with possibilities and opportunities.

Human qualities such as curiosity, creativity, humor, ingenuity, resourcefulness, spirituality, intuition and connection to others live beneath the skin of our physical vehicles. Qualities that are unknown, forgotten and/or rejected also exist. We may lose connection to parts of ourselves out of fear of minimization or rejection by others. Sometimes these qualities are attached to certain memories—and the memories evoke strong emotions, so they are pushed away defensively. In the creative process, we experience increased awareness and appreciation of the diversity of our body-vehicles, and learn to travel the journey of life with joyful participation in our own life stories. The act of valuing the uniqueness of self, inside and outside, gives our lives greater meaning and purpose.

The current trend to hyper-focus on *how* a body-vehicle appears to others has resulted in a reduction in the quality of the journey itself. When resources of time, money and attention to the appearance of the body-vehicle are exhausted, there is less opportunity to experience and appreciate events that take place within the diverse story-lines of our lives. Strict attention paid to our physical mode of transport, beyond what is practical for the journey, distracts from attention to qualities that drive movement and growth in our lives. Once we come to know ourselves deeply and completely, acceptance and appreciation follow. With greater faith and self-confidence in personal qualities and abilities, we face challenges rather than avoid them. The life journey, made up of self-authored stories, has potential for adventure, opportunity, fun, endurance, resiliency and connection to people and places in the world.

The opportunity for women to explore the many parts of self that come together to form the whole is a theme woven into all the experientials contained in this book. During the "Heads and Tales" experiential, participants continue to learn about themselves—thoughts and feelings are explored and validated by the facilitator, clinician and/or group. A non-judgemental approach to self-exploration and self-evaluation is reinforced and women benefit from the cumulative effect of creative engagement, verbal processing, reinforcement of self-exploration and positive self-evaluation. Women experience growth and transformation as they come to understand and believe that negative body image has *something* to do with the actual physical body but is more profoundly affected by lack of connection to the world of self beneath the skin. Qualities of self, found in our inner world, play out in the stories of our lives.

The epic tales of our lives are comprised of shorter stories that we have lived out, or that have yet to be lived out. We may imagine a bookshelf in our mind that holds these storybooks. The accounts of birth and death are the bookends, with dramas, comedies, romances, thrillers, mysteries, fantasies and adventures in between. Some books are positioned so that they are easily accessible and can be quickly removed from the shelf as we recount the episodes of our lives. Other books may be positioned on the shelf so they are not easily accessible; they collect a protective dust that clouds the sensory recall of people and events. Books with blank pages also sit on the shelves; these books exist for the tales we have yet to live out, the potential for joys and sorrows, disappointments and accomplishments, loves gained and lost.

As we contemplate the future stories of our lives, with a deeper appreciation of our internal and external selves, we are open to greater opportunity for movement and growth. When a woman cultivates a vision of what is needed from the body to live a meaningful life, she is able to release unrealistic expectations that sustain self-doubt. The human body, with all of its abilities and limitations, moves us through our life adventures. In reflecting on what is needed or desired we consider: mobility, flexibility, strength, endurance, sensory abilities and overall health of the system. When we bring these qualities together, we are able to develop a "body for life." The image of the body, placed in an imagined story, comes to life and affects the overall perception of self.

The "Heads and Tales" experiential presents particular challenges, as well as potential benefits if those challenges are faced and overcome. This process requires a photograph of each participant's face or head. I have experienced resistance from some women who perceive any image of self in a negative way. This resistance is typically resolved as participants are reminded of ways that anxiety can be expressed and managed. Before the process begins, I remind participants of the multi-sensory approach to calming anxiety. For example, one participant identified a vase of flowers in the room that she could look at to distract her from the thoughts that provoked a heightened system response. Another woman stepped outside to feel the cool air on her skin and smell the flowers, when she felt overwhelmed by emotions. Awareness of the natural, multi-sensory, built-in response system brings a greater appreciation of the body. An important lesson is learned: strong emotions occur within the system; strong emotions can be calmed by the body's built-in response system. This system can be accessed quickly, particularly when practiced.

The process begins by asking participants to imagine something that they would like to do in their lives. This may involve a job, a relationship, a trip, a hobby, a spiritual practice or anything that involves the physical body as well as other aspects of the self. There tends to be a great variation in what women choose for this directive. Participants are then asked to identify the qualities of the physical body that would be required for this activity. The physical body does not exist in a vacuum; therefore, the internal qualities of self that drive the system are also explored. This may be the first time, in a very long time, that some group members have looked at the body beyond physical appearance. Members are encouraged to look beyond their own physical, emotional and intellectual limitations, real or imagined. Any qualities that are necessary for the activity and do not actually exist within the woman may be compensated for with other qualities of self. Every woman will face some limitations—there are no exceptions to that. Limitations are opportunities to see and experience ourselves in different ways.

During one workshop, the idea of mobility was addressed. One group member stood up and demonstrated the incredible ability of her arms and legs to bend at the joints and move in different directions. She pointed out that this is a body quality that she relies upon, but takes for granted. Another group member acknowledged symptoms of stiffness and lack of mobility caused by rheumatoid arthritis—she imagined herself sitting in a carriage moving through Central Park in a horse-drawn carriage, connecting to the world with her smile, her voice and a poem that she would write to detail the experience.

After participants have identified something that they would like to do in their life, they are asked to bring the experience to life in an artistic rendition. The woman who imagined herself moving through Central Park in a carriage used a variety of art materials and techniques to reflect that experience. She collaged, stamped, painted and glitter-glued an image of herself sitting on board the carriage, smiling and waving to people around her. Actual photographs of each member's face or head are placed onto the paper. The face or head may be added to the picture at any time during the process.

I have handled the face or head shots required for this experiential in different ways. During a time when I owned a Polaroid camera, I took photos of the face or head of each participant during the workshop. This process was particularly beneficial for those who forgot to bring their pictures, or who decided at the last minute that they would be open to using a picture. (A number of women have arrived for group stating that they "forgot" their picture.) The major disadvantage of taking the picture during the process was the lack of selection of facial expressions to choose from (I took one or two pictures per person). When women know ahead of time what the process will involve, then they can bring a variety of face or head shots to place onto their picture. I keep a digital camera on hand for women who forget their pictures. The digital photos are transformed by my computer and printed out. If this technology is not available, participants may be asked to draw their faces or heads. They may replace these drawings with actual images when they are available. It is important to use an image of self to enhance the projective qualities of the image.

I have discovered that, once women engage in this art process, it becomes a joyful experience. This creative process initiates release and relief from painful and repetitive thoughts related to body dissatisfaction and other negative self-schemas. Curiosity, laughter and a sense of amazement are often expressed during the process.

Participants are asked to write a tale about the experience depicted in their artwork. They are reminded to incorporate the physical qualities of their body, as well as other qualities of self that helped to make the experience possible. If physical, emotional and/or cognitive challenges were faced, how were they overcome? Attention to the overall health of the body, mind and spirit enters into discussions;

these are explored as exciting enhancements of life experiences, rather than requirements for cultural acceptance. The seeds of motivation to work towards the health of body, mind and spirit are sown.

EXPERIENTIAL

Theme

Participants continue their life journeys, exploring resources and qualities of self beneath the skin. This process cultivates willingness and ability to see self beyond the realms of personal and societal limitations, to create a body that is needed for life. We are able to write tales of our lives that take place within our life journeys. Greater understanding and appreciation of our bodies leads to increased self-confidence and optimism as we explore the possibilities that lie before us.

Metaphors

The physical body is explored as a *vehicle* that moves participants through the storylines of their lives.

By tapping into cognitive, creative, emotional, intuitive and spiritual resources, participants develop or strengthen their identity as *authors* of their own life stories.

The *tales*, or stories, represent desires and possibilities that may occur during our lifetimes.

Objectives

- Introduce a multi-sensory approach to manage anxiety, which may occur during the art process.

- Address resistance related to use of a photo of face or head.

- Discuss the blend of reality-based thinking and imagination as a highly effective approach to problem solving.

- Discuss the benefits of a non-judgemental approach to exploration of self. (Allow for a creative, spiritual, intuitive approach.)

- Taking a non-judgemental approach, participants identify the strengths and limitations of their own physical body.

- Participants explore the qualities of self beneath the skin that affect the function of the body-vehicle: intelligence, creativity, humor, etc.

- Participants imagine something that they would like to do in life (imagined life experience). Because this is an *imagined* life experience, it can be *anything* that is desired.

- Participants consider internal and external *strength* factors specifically related to this imagined life experience.

- Participants consider internal and external *limitation* factors specifically related to this imagined life experience.

- Participants consider internal and external qualities that they would *like* to possess to fulfill this imagined life experience. Could these qualities be learned or cultivated? If not, what other internal or external qualities may *compensate* for the desired qualities?

- Use of a variety of art materials to reflect the imagined life experience. Participants are directed to include an image of the entire body, with the face or head photo attached.

- Development of a story that describes the imagined life experience depicted in the artwork. Use of a multi-sensory approach when describing the experience.

- Group discussion to explore processes and final images.

- Reinforce an ongoing awareness of, and appreciation for, our "body for life."

Settings

INITIAL DISCUSSION

Participants will require seating for initial discussion. Consider placing chairs in a circle so that group members can see each other during interactions. They should be provided with some type of hard surface (e.g. clipboard, notebook) to take notes. You may also request (ahead of time) that participants bring a notebook to the workshop.

Art Process

Participants will require adequate workspace to develop their images. An easily accessible table for art materials is desirable. The table should be set away from the wall, if possible, so that members can walk around the table to explore art materials. I suggest setting up a separate workstation for the warm glue gun.

Group Discussion

Same as the initial discussion setting.

- Music: It has become increasingly common for group members to request use of their own MP3 players during art processes. This is fine as long as the music is not disruptive to the group (some music can be heard outside of the headphones). I encourage the group to choose the type of music (if any) they would like to listen to during the process. I have a large selection of instrumental music.

- Art materials: Participants will need paper, pens and/or pencils to take notes and write stories. Art materials may include (but are not limited to): glue, glue guns, glitter glue, paints, markers, colored pencils, colored and decorative papers, broad selection of magazines for collage, travel brochures, postcards, tissue, cloth and any other desired materials. Participants are aware of the experiential ahead of time, and may bring any images or objects that they would like to include in the process.

1. Multi-Sensory Emotional Soothing

The brain can be *tricked* out of the distress response mode when it is exposed to any type of pleasure in the environment. For example, interest in something that brings laughter or joy will distract the brain from thoughts that trigger heightened anxiety, even the fight or flight response. I keep a few items such as joke books and books containing funny images in a section of the room for instant distraction. A simple poster or photo with a humorous image or expression may be placed on the wall somewhere in the room. Here are examples of multi-sensory items that help to soothe and distract:

- tactile: Slinky, play-dough, Newton's Cradle, a bowl of marbles or beans to run the hands through.

- visual: A scene outside the window, magic eye poster, theme books, an aquarium.

- olfactory: Small bags containing fresh baked cookies, herbs such as rosemary, soaps or candles.

- sound: Small instruments that can be used outdoors or in another room, MP3 players.

- taste: Sweet and sour candies, chocolate, fruit, crunchy foods (carrots), gum and teas.

> There are many ways that you can take care of yourself if you begin to feel anxious, or experience strong emotions during the process. The techniques are simple and effective. Sometimes just taking deep breaths and feeling yourself grounded as you sit in your chair, or standing, will help to reduce the stress response mode.
>
> Take a few moments to look at the items in the room. Feel free to use them if anxiety or other emotional responses detract from the quality of your process.

2. Approaches to Problem Solving

> You will find yourself in problem solving mode at different times throughout this experiential. This is a time for you to keep an open mind; imagine that you are seeing challenges through the eyes of an artist. Feel the joy of resolutions that come from a blend of realistic thinking and fantastical approaches to problem solving. Realistic thoughts come from our ability to reason; fantasy thoughts come from the world of the imagination.

3. Taking a Non-Judgemental Approach to Exploration of Self

> This is an opportunity for you to release the negative thoughts of self you are experiencing or holding. Imagine those thoughts and feelings floating away on the clouds, or drifting away on the waves of the ocean. You are seeing yourself today through the eyes of an artist—you are the artist. Pay attention to creative thoughts and ideas; write them down or sketch them out on paper. Listen to your intuition and the voice of wisdom from deep within; draw from your spirituality as you explore the mystery of yourself unfolding.

4. Identifying Strengths and Limitations of the Physical Body

Every human being experiences strengths and limitations of the physical body. Make a list of physical qualities of your own body that you consider to be strengths. Consider attributes associated with mobility, flexibility, strength, endurance, resiliency, sensory abilities and overall health of the system.

Now make a list of physical qualities of your own body that you consider to be limitations. Consider attributes associated with the ones listed above. Remember that limitations (perceived or real) are opportunities to see and experience ourselves in a different way.

5. Looking at Qualities of Self Beneath the Skin

It is time to look beneath the skin to explore qualities of self that truly drive the movement of the body-vehicle through the life journey. Think about the many qualities that contribute to who you are: intelligence, creativity, ingenuity, humor, curiosity, resourcefulness, intuition, resiliency, spirituality and connection to others are just a few.

You may associate yourself with some traits that are valued and appreciated by yourself and others; some may be untapped resources yet to be explored. Imagine the incredible things that you can do in this life if you believe in yourself.

6. Imagined Life Experience

Imagine something that you would like to do on this life journey. Try not to limit yourself when considering the possibilities for this *imagined life experience*. You are the author of this life story—make the most of it. The imagined life experience you choose may involve an event, a trip, a hobby, a relationship, a job, a spiritual practice or anything that involves the physical body as well as qualities of self found beneath the skin. You may choose an extraordinary feat such as travel into space, discovery of a cure for a disease, or being in a position to end a war. There are challenging experiences to consider, such as skydiving, rock climbing or painting a mural on the outside of a building. You may desire an adventure such as swimming with dolphins, trying your hand at stand-up comedy or studying a culture in another part of the world. Your imagined life experience may involve a relationship with a person you know, or hope to know someday. You could meet the President of the United States, your favorite politician or musician, or a loved one who lives far away. The life experience may be simpler: walking your dog, taking (and passing!) an exam, planting a garden. The possibilities for this imagined life experience are limitless. This is an opportunity to create and overcome challenges; try to remain open to any experiences that come to mind.

7. Internal and External Strengths for Imagined Life Experience

This is a time to reflect on the internal and external strengths that you have identified so far; consider which ones would be helpful for your imagined life experience.

8. Internal and External Limitations for Imagined Life Experience

Taking a non-judgemental approach, consider the physical, emotional, cognitive and/or spiritual limitations that could affect your imagined life experience. Remember that your limitations do not define you; understanding them leads to knowing yourself more completely.

9. Qualities You Would Like to Have for this Experience

Let your imagination take the lead as you envision internal and external qualities of self that you would like to have for this life experience. Again taking a non-judgemental approach, reflect on the existence of these features within yourself. Do they seem to be a part of who you are? If not, can you imagine developing the qualities? If these features seem particularly challenging, then consider other qualities that may help compensate for what is needed to develop your story. Reflect on the importance of establishing and maintaining overall health of body, mind and spirit.

Art Process

The image created in this art process may be considered as the *illustration* for your developing story. It is a snapshot of what you see, as you visualize yourself engaging in the experience that you imagined.

Using a variety of art materials, depict yourself in your imagined life experience. The picture should somehow reflect your physical body, as well as qualities of self found beneath the skin. Keep in mind everything that you have considered about yourself; however, there are no limits to what you can bring to the process. Remember to blend reason with imagination to create the most expansive conceptualization of the experience.

Writing Process

Bring your picture to life with a story! Imagine that the picture you created is a snapshot of a moment in time. What led up to this moment? What happened after this moment? Use a multi-sensory approach to include sights, sounds, smells, tastes and tactile sensations in the context of the story. Maintain a non-judgemental perspective as you describe how both internal and external qualities of self affect what is taking place in the experience.

Dialogue and Reflection Process

Possible questions for discussion:

- Tell the story depicted in your picture.

- How did the physical qualities of self play into the story?

- How did the qualities of self beneath the skin play into the story?

- What did you discover about yourself in this process?

- Is the experience depicted in the image representative of a *meaningful life*? Why, or why not?

- Discuss your impression of the overall health of your body, mind and spirit.

- What would you like to continue to work on, or explore?

- Are there any new possibilities that you see for your life journey?

Homework

Place your picture in a visible location. As you look at the image, remember your imagined life experience. Remember the role your body plays in this experience. Continue to explore your internal and external resources that will help to bring your experience to life.

Heads and Tales

Artist's Statement

This piece is about my conflicted future. In my drawing I have included images of how I see myself in the future. I know I am going to have to work my ass off. I always put trees in my pictures to represent strength. The fish is a protector. In this drawing, I am pregnant. I have to take care of my body so I can do the work I want to do, and carry my baby.

Figure 13.1 What I see

Figure 13.2 Mind, body, spirit

References

Borysenko, J. (1996) *A Woman's Book of Life: The Biology, Psychology, and Spirituality of the Feminine Life Cycle.* New York: Riverhead Books.

Campbell, J. (2008) *The Hero with a Thousand Faces.* Third edition. Novato, CA: New World Library. (Originally published 1949.)

Cash, T.F. and Fleming, E.C. (2004) "Body Image and Social Relations." In T.F. Cash and T. Pruzinsky (eds) *Image: A Handbook of Theory, Research, and Clinical Practice.* New York: Guilford Press.

Costin, C. (2007) *The Eating Disorder Source Book.* Third edition. New York: McGraw-Hill.

Cummings, L. (2003) "The Diet Business: Banking on Failure." Accessed on 22 November 2011 at www.media-awareness.ca/english/issues/stereotyping/women_and_girls/women_beauty.cfm

Dissanayake, E. (1992) *Homo Aestheticus.* Seattle: University of Washington Press.

Gillespie, J. (1994) *The Projective Use of Mother-and-Child Drawings: A Manual for Clinicians.* New York: Brunner/Mazel.

Grogan, S. (2008) *Understanding Body Dissatisfaction in Men, Women and Children.* Second edition. New York: Routledge.

Hari, J. (2009) "The Fashion Industry Imposes a Cruel Burden on Women: The Prison of the Unachievable Body Shape has Replaced the Prison of the Kitchen." Accessed on 15 November 2011 at www.independent.co.uk/opinion/commentators/johann-hari/johann-hari-the-fashion-industry-imposes-a-cruel-burden-on-women-1787808.html

Hass-Cohen, N. (2008) "Partnering of Art Therapy and Clinical Neuroscience." In N. Hass-Cohen and R. Carr (eds) *Art Therapy and Clinical Neuroscience.* London: Jessica Kingsley Publishers.

Johnston, A. (1996) *Eating in the Light of the Moon.* Carlsbad, CA: Gurze Books.

Kabat-Zinn, J. (1993) "Meditation." In B. Moyers, *Healing and the Mind.* New York: Doubleday.

Kabat-Zinn, J. (2003) "Mindfulness-based interventions in context: Past, present and future." *Clinical Psychology: Science and Practice 10,* 2, 144–156.

Kearney-Cooke, A. (2002) "Familial Influence on Body Image Development." In T.F. Cash and T. Pruzinsky (eds) *Body Image: A Handbook of Theory, Research, and Clinical Practice.* New York: Guilford Press.

Korb, P., Davenport, J. and Korb, J.P. (1996) "Creativity." The Gestalt Center of Gainesville. Accessed on 16 November 2011 at www.afb.org/~gestalt/creative.htm

Kravits, K. (2008) "The Neurobiology of Relatedness Attachment." In N. Hass-Cohen and R. Carr (eds) *Art Therapy and Clinical Neuroscience.* London: Jessica Kingsley Publishers.

Krueger, D. (2004) "Psychodynamic Perspectives on Body Image." In T.F. Cash and T. Pruzinsky (eds) *Body Image: A Handbook of Theory, Research, and Clinical Practice.* New York: Guilford Press.

Levine, M.P. and Smolak, L. (2004) "Body Image Development in Adolescence." In T.F. Cash and T. Pruzinsky (eds) *Body Image: A Handbook of Theory, Research, and Clinical Practice.* New York: Guilford Press.

Malchiodi, C. (2007) *The Art Therapy Sourcebook.* New York: McGraw-Hill.

Merriam-Webster's Online Dictionary (2012) "Inspiration." Accessed on 8 Febuary 2012 at www.merriam-webster.com/dictionary/inspiration

Moon, C.H. (2002) *Studio Art Therapy: Cultivating the Artist Identity in the Art Therapist.* London: Jessica Kingsley Publishers.

Moon, C.H. (2010) *Materials and Media in Art Therapy: Critical Understanding of Diverse Artistic Vocabularies.* New York: Routledge.

National Alliance on Mental Illness (NAMI) (2010) Accessed on 12 April at www.nami.org/content/navigationMenu/Mental_Illness/Women_and_Depression/womenanddepression.pdf

National Centre for Eating Disorders (2009) "Body Image." Accessed on 12 April 2012 at www.eating-disorders.org.uk/body-image.html

Northrup, C. (1998) *Women's Bodies, Women's Wisdom: Creating Physical and Emotional Health and Healing* (revised). New York: Bantam.

Orbach, S. (2007) "Interview with Susie Orbach." *Figure: Demystifying the Feminist Mystique: A Feminist Blog from Both Sides of the Pond.* Accessed on 27 November 2011 at http://feministfigure.blogspot.com/2007/04/interview-with-susie-orbach.html

Renfrew Center Foundation for Eating Disorders (2002) "Eating Disorders 101 Guide: A Summary of Issues, Statistics and Resources." Accessed on 6 March 2012 at www.renfrew.org

Richardson, K. (2010) "Keeping Us Fat: Why Not Losing Weight is Profitable." www.naturallyintense.net/blog/weight-loss/keeping-us-fat-why-not-losing-weight-is-profitable

Schnetz, M. (2005) *The Healing Flow: Artistic Expression in Therapy Creative Arts and the Process of Healing. An Image/Word Approach Inquiry.* London: Jessica Kingsley Publishers.

Smolak, L. (2004) "Body Image Development in Children." In T.F. Cash and T. Pruzinsky (eds) *Body Image: A Handbook of Theory, Research, and Clinical Practice.* New York: Guilford Press.

Thompson, J.K., Heinberg, L.J., Altabe, M. and Tantleff-Dunn, S. (1999) *Exacting Beauty: Theory, Assessment, and Treatment of Body Image Disturbances.* New York: Guilford Press.

Wadeson, H. (1987) "An Eclectic Approach to Art Therapy." In J.A. Rubin (ed.) *Approaches to Art Therapy: Theory and Technique.* New York: Brunner/Mazel.

Williamson, D. Stewart, T., White, M. and York-Crowe, E. (2002) "An Information-Processing Perspective on Body Image." In T.F. Cash and T. Pruzinsky (eds) *Body Image: A Handbook of Theory, Research, and Clinical Practice.* New York: Guilford Press.

Winterman, D. (2009) "What Would a Real Life Barbie Look Like?" Accessed on 6 March 2012 at http://news.bbc.co.uk/z/hi/uk_news/magazine/7920962.stm

Wolfe, N. (2002) *The Beauty Myth: How Images of Beauty Are Used Against Women.* New York: HarperCollins.

Index